Paula Denton
Roxann Kriete

All net proceeds from the sale of this book support the work of Northeast Foundation for Children, Inc. (NEFC). NEFC, a not-for-profit educational organization, is the developer of the *Responsive Classroom*® approach to teaching, which fosters safe, challenging, and joyful elementary classrooms and schools.

The stories in this book are all based on real events in the classroom. However, in order to respect the privacy of students, names and many identifying characteristics of students and situations have been changed.

ISBN: 978-1-892989-04-8

Library of Congress catalog card number 00-100105

Photographs: Peter Wrenn, Marlynn K. Clayton, William Elwell, and Cherry Wyman

Cover and book design: Woodward Design

NORTHEAST FOUNDATION FOR CHILDREN, INC.
85 Avenue A, Suite 204
P. O. Box 718
Turners Falls, MA 01376-0718
800-360-6332
www.responsiveclassroom.org

14 13 12 11 17 16 15

Printed on recycled paper.

We would like to thank the Shinnyo-en Foundation for its generous support of the development of this book.

The mission of the Shinnyo-en Foundation is "to bring forth deeper compassion among humankind, to promote greater harmony, and to nurture future generations toward building more caring communities."

ACKNOWLEDGMENTS

The ideas in this book spring from the work of all who created and continue to contribute to the *Responsive Classroom*® approach to teaching and learning. We note the vital role played by our colleagues at Northeast Foundation for Children who generously shared their thoughts, offered encouragement and critique, welcomed us into their classrooms, and trusted us to interpret and articulate their work. Directly and indirectly, many of their words, ideas, and practices are present in this book.

Specifically, we want to thank:

Mary Beth Forton for her astute judgments and clarity, her quiet persistence, and her ability to persuade a very shaggy project to follow a timeline. Her work enriched every aspect of the book.

Jay Lord for helping conceive the Strategies for Teachers series and securing funding for it. In his inimitable fashion, he transformed a tedious research task into a fun project, documenting songs, games, and stories that added immensely to the usefulness of this book.

Chip Wood for reading the manuscript and using his broad knowledge of the current educational arena to comment upon and strengthen it.

Ruth Charney for offering words of encouragement and illuminating insights about classrooms.

Marlynn Clayton for teaching us much about the value of a patient, deliberate introduction to the school year.

Deborah Porter, who unstintingly shared much wisdom from her years working with both children and teachers. She informed and inspired the primary grades section.

Terry Kayne, careful reader, for making many valuable suggestions based on ideas from her warm and lively second grade classroom.

Susan Pelis for sharing specific, successful strategies and materials she uses with kindergarten and first grade students.

Jane Stephenson for contributing wonderful samples of scavenger hunts and student surveys from her third and fourth grade classroom.

The teachers and students from many schools who opened their classrooms and shared aspects of their school lives with us during the past several years.

The parents and children of Greenfield Center School, formerly NEFC's laboratory school, whose trust and participation over the past twenty years has enabled the development of *The Responsive Classroom* approach.

Leslie and Jeff Woodward, designers, for bringing their consistently high level of competence, their pleasure in collaboration, and a sense of fun to this project.

Laurie Euvrard for carefully and competently handling so many details of this project, from pulling together the bibliography to curing computer viruses and coordinating printing.

Allen Woods, clear-eyed and skillful editor, who made several key suggestions that organized and shaped the manuscript.

Judith Bellamy, proofreader, for bringing consistency and care to the details of these pages.

Nancy Ratner for her specific observations and enthusiasm early in the writing process.

Len Lubinsky, executive director of NEFC, for encouraging us to take the time needed to get things right, even when that meant missed meetings and altered schedules.

NEFC's Board of Directors, whose members give so generously of their skills and resources to help Northeast Foundation for Children grow into a stable, healthy organization.

Paula also thanks *Dr. Masha Rudman* for her helpful feedback and support and sends special appreciation to Steve for his patience and listening ear.

Roxann appreciates the support and companionship of her colleagues in NEFC's publishing branch—*Mary Beth, Laurie, Jean, Jay, Bonnie, and Mike.* She thanks *Russ, Ben, and Rachel, as well as her extended family,* for their love and support, expressed in so many ways.

TABLE OF CONTENTS

Who is Talking?

A Note to Our Readers

This book is full of the ideas, strategies, and specific suggestions of many teachers, including but far exceeding those of the co-authors. In writing this book, we struggled with the question of voice. It seemed confusing to always say "we," presumptuous to say "you," and impersonal to say "the teacher."

For simplicity, we decided to use a collective "I" as the voice of the teacher in each of the rooms we describe. We also use the first person when telling a story that is clearly unique and personal to the speaker.

In describing the theories and reasoning behind our approach to the early weeks of school, "we" seemed to be the best choice to indicate a group which includes the authors as well as many others who have used and improved these techniques.

Prime Factors

AN INTRODUCTION

Mid-morning winter sun streams through the southern windows of the room. It is one of those idyllic moments in the life of a classroom, the mood harmonious and full of industry. I am sitting at a table with Megan, going over the math lesson on prime factors that she missed yesterday.

Introduction

The background noise is a pleasant hum—a blend of voices in carefully modulated conversation, pencils tracking across paper, and the heater's steady purr. As Megan concentrates, I take a moment to survey the room.

Chris, Leisha, Andrew, and Jon are sharing our one globe as they search it to locate and write two facts about each of the four countries mentioned in current events yesterday. A brief burst of laughter punctuates the literature group, meeting in the opposite corner of the room with Ms. W., a special needs teacher who supports our language arts work. Jenna reenters the room, moving her nametag from the bathroom hook to the wicker basket on the small shelf below. Luis is in the library corner, immersed in the latest Harry Potter fantasy.

Many things are going on in this fourth grade classroom at the same time: one-to-one instruction, teacher-facilitated small group instruction, individual independent work, and collaborative student work. The students are drawing upon many resources for their learning, including each other. It is a classroom in which many learning styles are honored and students at varying levels of proficiency are being challenged.

Luis is known for his love of reading and quick recall of details. Andrew is a mechanical wonder and the first one we all look to when the pencil sharpener jams or the cassette player won't play. Chris does pen and ink sketches with a sophisticated perspective and artistic flair, and her classmates have begun to seek her out for this talent. In fact, first thing this morning I heard Anna consulting her about the book poster she was trying to finish for literature group: "My drawing's a mess, Chris. Can you help me make this road look right?"

I watched with satisfaction as Chris smiled a hesitant, shy smile, looked Anna almost in the eye, and responded, "Sure, but could I get my backpack off first?" Chris was new to the class in November and spent the first month trying her hardest to say little and hide often. More than once, I coaxed her from the girls' room back to class.

Although there is much activity and many materials are in use, there is a sense of order, and the adults are free to focus on instruction and observation. The room is very much in control as students function with a great deal of nine-year-old autonomy.

Prime Factors

Megan's voice ends my brief survey, and my attention returns to the math at hand. She has finished the first problem and asks, "So, did I get it? Are these the prime factors?"

The foundations for such idyllic moments of concentrated and varied learning are built in the early weeks of school each year. It is during this time that we spell out expectations, articulate rules, and establish predictable structures, all of which provide the "prime factors" which help us move toward an orderly, cooperative, and stimulating learning environment.

They help us handle the inevitable moments of upset and disorder as well. In the scene above, Andrew may spin the globe faster and faster until the rest of the group grows frustrated and Andrew stomps off in a huff. Jenna may linger in the bathroom until I find her and Amy composing an anonymous note to Courtney detailing why "no one" likes her. Jon and Jermaine may fight on the playground. The expectations, rules, and structures established during the first weeks prepare us—teachers and children—to handle these situations constructively. They become opportunities for learning.

Improving the learning environment requires asking—and answering—a critical question: What must our students know in order to be a part of a cooperative, rigorous, and supportive classroom community?

Much knowledge and many skills are required. Students must know how to leave the room without interrupting the teacher or other students, while letting the teacher know where they are at all times. They must know how loud "indoor voices" can be. They must know what information they can find out from a globe. They must know how four people can share one globe and how to (and not to) handle it. They must know something of their classmates' strengths and fragilities. They must know how to ask each other for help. They must know how to get to literature group quickly and efficiently with the materials they will need. They must know how to put the special drawing pencils back in the art cans so that they will be there for the next student who needs them.

In a word, students need to function with autonomy: to function independently without constant adult control or direct supervision. Autonomy in a school setting means governing oneself with an awareness of the needs of the community. These needs vary—each year, each month, each week—according to the class composition, students' maturity, what our classroom space allows, and what materials we have to work with.

Even the best-behaved students do not walk in our doors in September with this autonomy. Each year, the details must be intentionally established during the first weeks, bit by specific bit, through definition and constant practice. Some students will acquire a high degree of autonomy relatively quickly; others will struggle and need support all year long.

The "ideal" classroom moment described above reflects freedoms, choices, and responsibilities which are the result of students' ability to govern themselves—to draw upon individual self-controls that will enable the whole group to function smoothly.

Intentions

Though the details differ with different age groups, with the content of the curriculum, and with the organization of the room, there are four broad aims—four prime factors—in our first six weeks curriculum.

Intentions During the First Six Weeks:

1. **Create a climate and tone of warmth and safety.**
2. **Teach the schedule and routines of the school day and our expectations for behavior in each of them.**

3. **Introduce students to the physical environment and materials of the classroom and the school, and teach students how to use and care for them.**

4. **Establish expectations about ways we will learn together in the year ahead.**

Intentions

1. Create a climate and tone of warmth and safety.

Students can come to know each other and develop a sense of belonging through activities that help them define their commonality and their differences. Deliberately focusing on group-building helps create the trust essential for active, collaborative learning.

However, this sense of trust isn't built solely on warmth and friendliness. It is also built upon students' assurance that there are reasonable limits and boundaries for behavior and that their teacher will enforce them. They must see that their teacher will exercise vigilance and good judgment to keep everyone safe.

2. Teach the schedule and routines of the school day and our expectations for behavior in each of them.

A sense of order and predictability in daily school life is important. It enables children to relax, to focus their energy on learning, and to feel competent. When we enter a new culture, we want to know its rules so that we do not embarrass ourselves or, through ignorance or misunderstanding, hurt others.

In the first weeks of school, we name the global expectations we hold for the year: our room will be a place where people try hard, take good care of themselves and each other, and take good care of our materials and facilities. Children are then involved in applying these broad, nonnegotiable expectations to everyday situations. "How will we move through the halls if we are taking care of each other?" "What does trying hard mean during math group?" "What will clean-up time look like if we are taking good care of our room?"

3. Introduce students to the physical environment and materials of the classroom and the school, and teach students how to use and care for them.

In order for students to feel a sense of ownership for the school environment and materials, they must become familiar with them and have time to explore them.

Through school tours for young students and new students, and scavenger hunts and mapping exercises for older ones, we encourage them to get acquainted or reacquainted with the school environment and to feel comfortable in it. Using the technique of guided discoveries, we extend children's ideas about the creative use of space and materials, develop guidelines about sharing particular resources, and teach children how to care for them.

4. Establish expectations about ways we will learn together in the year ahead.

We want to generate excitement and enthusiasm about the curricula we will engage in this year—complicated new math concepts, engrossing novels full of dilemmas to explore, beautiful art materials and techniques for using them, microscopes to observe a previously invisible world. Our learning—whether we are wrestling with an ethical dilemma presented in a history lesson, deciding when to pass the soccer ball, or considering a complicated question about collecting data for an experiment about the effects of caffeine—requires participation and focused effort, thoughtful questions, and the ability to cooperate and collaborate. We pay attention to the process as well as the products of our learning and hold high standards in both areas. It is our job as teachers to help students achieve these high standards as we learn with and from each other.

Introductions

The first six weeks of school is a distinct period: it is a time of many introductions. We introduce students to the people of the classroom and school community, to the classroom and school environment, and to the expectations we hold about learning. We also introduce and establish expectations for their behavior, the limits we will set, and the ways we will enforce those limits. We introduce the routines that help them learn while taking care of each other and the environment.

We structure the first six weeks so that students will participate actively in all of these introductions. They practice the expected skills and behaviors—at first with very close teacher guidance and structure, and then, as their familiarity and competence grow, with increasing amounts of independence. We want them to consider and voice their hopes and goals for the school year and to help articulate a set of rules that will help each one achieve their individual hopes and goals.

How long does this "first weeks" phase last? We have found that it almost always takes six weeks, though there is nothing exact or magic about the number six. Occasionally a class accomplishes the objectives of this phase in less time. Sometimes it takes longer. Paula recalls an exhausting year when "It was the first six weeks all year long." The group she had that year never stopped needing the structures and the vigilant attention to process and routine that define the first weeks.

This does not mean that academic goals are put on hold during this introductory period. Nor does the early-weeks curriculum compete with academic aims. On the contrary, these aims are intertwined and synergistic. Establishing a friendly, predictable, and orderly classroom is a prerequisite for children's academic achievement. When children are anxious, unruly, and out of control, the learning that occurs is seldom what we intend.

Introductions

We must convey, from the very first day, the important message that we will tackle challenging material and do high-quality work in our classroom. But we also must convey that we will tackle this material and do this high-quality work in an atmosphere of support and collaboration. This atmosphere will not just appear by our decree. It must be carefully constructed upon many small, but critical, building blocks.

The answers to the question posed earlier—What must our students know in order for them to achieve high-standard academic goals in an atmosphere of safety and cooperation?—are the source for these building blocks. The answers involve behavior and skills of many types and involve every aspect of the classroom environment.

For example, students must know each other's names. They must know what first-draft work looks like and what final-draft work looks like. They must know how loud their voices can be when a reading group is going on in the room. They must know that no one will laugh if their Fimo® duck is blob-like or their foot doesn't connect with the soccer ball every time. They must know what their choices are when they finish their math assignment early. They must know that a friendly "Good Morning" or a "Will you eat with me?" to a new student is noted and appreciated. They must know that a sneering response to a classmate's mispronounced vocabulary word is also noted and not appreciated.

Constructing and placing these building blocks are the focus of our curriculum for the early weeks of school. It is exhilarating and exhausting work. It is an investment that pays off all year long.

Using This Book

In this book we describe the specific goals of each of the first six weeks of school, and the strategies which help us accomplish the four broad aims stated in the introduction.

The First Three Weeks

We offer sample daily schedules for the first three weeks to illustrate in very concrete terms how we engage in the lofty-sounding business of building community, creating a safe climate, and investing children in their learning.

Within the description of each of the first three weeks, there are three sets of plans: one for the primary grades (K–2), one for the middle elementary grades (3–4), and one for the upper elementary grades (5–6). After the daily schedules, we offer reflections about elements of our plans—what assumptions we make and, as importantly, don't make; what criteria inform our choices of games to play, books to read, and topics to study in these early weeks.

We offer these sample daily plans as templates only. They give a sense of the flavor, priorities, and pace that have worked for us. The details of these plans come from the contexts where we have taught and observed. Those details can and should change based upon your knowledge of your own context—your students, the academic curricula and approaches you use, the materials available to you, and your own teaching strengths and preferences.

There is nothing essential about studying spiders or reading a particular story on a particular day. There is much artistry in teaching and much room for interpretation and variation in the plans we outline. Acknowledging the wide variation in academic programs that different teachers and schools use, we refer to specific academic curricula and approaches in this book mainly to serve as illustrations of the ways we recommend introducing courses of study.

It is beyond the scope of this book to recommend specific curricula. Our audience includes teachers who are expected to use standardized curricula with specific requirements for how they will allot their instructional time as well as teachers who can exercise a significant amount of freedom in deciding what they will teach and when they will teach it. Readers will need to modify these plans (or create their own plans) based on the curricular requirements in their schools. Our primary objective here is to show an approach for introducing curricula that entails the careful introduction of learning materials and process and encourages active participation and engagement. More important than the specifics of what you teach is that the teaching holds meaning and a rich sense of purpose for the students.

Weeks Four to Six

During weeks four through six, the second phase of the year, we do not necessarily allocate our time differently from the remainder of the school year. Instead, within what will be our regular, ongoing schedule, we introduce some new strategies that continue to help children assume increasing degrees of responsibility and further their internalization of the expectations established in the first three weeks.

The format of Chapter Four (Weeks Four to Six), therefore, moves away from offering examples of daily schedules, and instead describes additional strategies and structures helpful in these weeks—various types of logical consequences, Class Meeting, and apology of action, for example. Unlike earlier chapters, this chapter contains no sub-divisions by grade level, since the strategies are applicable to all grade levels. As with any strategies, teachers will adjust language, time frames, and other elements based upon their knowledge of their class.

Key Terms

Some of the terminology we use has a particular definition and connotation in the *Responsive Classroom*® lexicon. Following this introduction are some definitions and elaborations upon terms—Morning Meeting and its components, guided discovery, and academic choice, for example—which may, for some readers, need more explanation than is embedded in the text itself. If you are not already conversant with the *Responsive Classroom* teaching practices, you may find it helpful to read this section first. You may also want to refer to it later.

Appendixes

Throughout the book, there are specific references to games, activities, songs, greetings, and read-aloud books for the first six weeks of school. You'll find complete descriptions of these in the appendixes along with further recommendations, coded with appropriate grade levels.

Wilson

Key Terms

Some of the terminology we use in this book has a particular definition and connotation in the *Responsive Classroom*® lexicon. In this section you will find definitions and elaborations upon key terms such as Morning Meeting and its components, guided discovery, and academic choice. If you are not already conversant with the *Responsive Classroom* teaching practices, you may find it helpful to read this section first.

The *Responsive Classroom* Approach

This approach to teaching and learning has grown out of the work of Northeast Foundation for Children (NEFC). NEFC's mission is to help schools become caring communities in which social and academic learning are fully integrated throughout the school day, and in which students are nurtured to become strong and ethical thinkers.

The following seven beliefs, based on developmental and social learning theory and informed by years of experience in the classroom, underlie the *Responsive Classroom* approach (Wood 1999, 293):

1. The social curriculum is as important as the academic curriculum. Social and academic learning are inextricably connected, and each is equally important. The balanced integration of the two is essential to children's growth.

2. How children learn is as important as what children learn. Children learn best when they have the opportunity to make choices about what they're learning and to make their own discoveries through trial and error. Ideally there should be a balance between teacher-directed and child-initiated experiences.

3. The greatest cognitive growth occurs through social interaction. While children certainly do learn when they are working alone—reading a book, taking a test, completing a worksheet—children learn the most when they are engaged in meaningful ways with others.

4. Children need a set of social skills in order to be successful academically and socially. These skills form the simple acronym CARES—cooperation, assertion, responsibility, empathy, and self-control—and should be taught in an integrated fashion throughout the school day.

5. Knowing the children we teach is as important as knowing the content we teach. The more known children feel at school, the more likely it is that they will succeed. Teachers come to know children individually, culturally, and developmentally by taking time to observe and interact with students and by understanding the stages of child development. The science of child development is the most important academic discipline for teachers.

The Responsive Classroom

Morning Meeting

6. Knowing the parents of the children we teach is as important as knowing the children. Parent involvement is essential to children's education. The greatest gains are made when educators work with parents as partners.

7. Teachers and administrators must model the social and academic skills which they wish to teach their students. These skills must be lived daily in educators' interactions with each other, with children, and with parents. Meaningful and lasting change for the better in our schools requires good working relationships among the adult community. Children are always watching.

Further Reading

- These seven principles of the *Responsive Classroom* are further defined and discussed in Chip Wood's book, *Time to Teach, Time to Learn: Changing the Pace of School.* Turners Falls, Mass.: Northeast Foundation for Children, 1999.

Morning Meeting

Morning Meeting is a twenty- to thirty-minute daily routine used to begin the school day in elementary and middle school classrooms. All classroom members—adults and children—gather in a circle to greet one another, to listen and respond to each other's news, to practice academic and social skills, and to look forward to the events in the day ahead.

The purposes of Morning Meeting are many. It serves as a transition from home to school, helps children to feel welcome and known, sets the tone for the day, creates a climate of trust, increases students' confidence and investment in learning, provides a meaningful context for teaching and practicing academic skills, encourages cooperation and inclusion, and improves children's communication skills.

Morning Meeting consists of four components:

1. *Greeting:* Children greet each other by name, often including handshaking, clapping, singing, and other activities.

2. *Sharing:* Students share some news of interest to the class and respond to each other, practicing communication skills and learning about one another.

3. *Group Activity:* The whole class does a short activity together, building class cohesion through active participation.

4. *Morning Message:* Students develop language skills and learn about the events in the day ahead by reading and discussing a daily message posted on a chart by their teacher. (For samples of morning message charts, see Appendix A.)

While the format is intentionally predictable, there is plenty of room for variation within this format. Meetings vary from teacher to teacher and class to class, each meeting reflecting the style and flavor of the individual teachers and groups.

Further Reading

- Kriete, Roxann. *The Morning Meeting Book.* Turners Falls, Mass.: Northeast Foundation for Children, 1999.

Guided Discovery

Guided discovery is a focused, purposeful, yet playful technique teachers use to introduce materials, areas, or activities to students. A teacher might use a guided discovery to introduce a learning center, such as the library or computer area; a specific material, such as a box of crayons or compass; or a process, such as journal writing or quiet time.

A teacher may have any of the following objectives in mind when doing a guided discovery:

- To excite and motivate children by exploring possibilities
- To stretch individual students toward involvement in new areas of learning
- To guide or deepen the understanding of materials and activities
- To encourage the sharing of ideas among children for how a material or area might be used
- To establish a common language and vocabulary
- To generate rules and procedures for the care of materials and spaces
- To teach or reinforce guidelines for working cooperatively

Format for a Guided Discovery

Guided Discovery

Generally, a guided discovery consists of five stages, or some variation of them, illustrated in the following example. A teacher is introducing pattern blocks to a group of kindergartners/first graders during the first few weeks of school. The whole group is sitting in a circle.

T: signifies what the teacher might say

C: signifies what the children might say

1. Introduction—naming

T: What do you think I have in this box? (Teacher rattles a small box containing one of each pattern block.) Who has an idea?

C: Rocks, crayons, blocks...

T: I do have blocks in here, but now can you guess more about them?

C: Is there a yellow one? Is there a square one? (Teacher brings out the blocks as children guess what else is inside and name the individual blocks. With older children, the teacher may ask for more information before bringing the blocks out. The guessing continues until all the blocks are revealed.)

T: What do you notice about these blocks?

C: Different colors, shapes, they're pretty, some are bigger...

This hiding of the object and guessing strategy is just one way to introduce and name the item. Teachers may choose to simply name the object/activity which they'll be introducing that day, especially with older students.

2. Generating ideas and modeling exploratory work

T: What can we do with these?

C: Build something.
T: Okay. (Teacher demonstrates making a design with blocks.) What do you notice?
C: It stands up. It looks like a...
T: What else could we do with these? (Teacher may want to model other ideas children suggest or have several children demonstrate other ideas and show various ways to build with the shapes.)
C: Make a pattern, building, tower...

3. Children explore

Teacher asks every child to take two of each shape of block and to work in a space in front of where the group is sitting. As the children are working, the role of the teacher is to observe, to reinforce the discoveries, to notice the positive social interactions and the care of materials, and to remind and redirect when children "forget."

Key Terms

T: Make a beautiful design. (Teacher allows about five minutes, then stops and asks children to share designs.)
T: Make another design. (Children keep experimenting.)
T: Make something high, something flat, something that has open spaces. Make an animal, a weird thing, a wall...(Teacher experiments with various ideas as long as the group remains focused. The length of time will vary, of course, at different grade levels.)

4. Children share their explorations and observations

After each guided instruction from the teacher, a few children (in a large group) or all children (in a small group) will share their work, and children will respond to the work of their peers.

Sharing: The teacher begins by asking a focusing question. For example, what is one thing you like about what you made, one thing you noticed, one thing that was hard, one thing that was tricky, etc.

T: Tell one thing that you like about your construction.
C: I like the red part, the top part, all of it...

Comments: Children respond to the work of their peers by telling one thing that they see or like.

T: Tell one thing that you like about ______'s design.
C: I like the way he did the windows. It looks like a...

5. Cleanup and care of materials

Teacher asks children to think about and show how they will care for the material or area.

T: Who can show us a careful and safe way to put all the blocks away in their container?

T: Who can show us what to do while waiting for the container?

T: Who can show us how they would pass the container when they are done?

T: What's another way we could put away the pattern blocks when lots of people are using them? (Someone gets all the circles, someone else will get the squares...)

T: Where is a good place for you to display your finished work?

Guided Discovery

Academic Choice

A guided discovery can be done with a whole group, a small subgroup, or individuals, and can be used to present both familiar and new resources. It is certainly not necessary for every material or every activity; teachers use it selectively. It is an invaluable tool for teaching children to use their environment and the things in it with respect, attention, and interest.

Further Reading

- Charney, Ruth S. *Teaching Children to Care: Classroom Management for Ethical and Academic Growth, K–8,* rev. ed. Turners Falls, Mass.: Northeast Foundation for Children, 2002.
- Charney, Ruth S. "Guided Discovery: Teaching the Freedom to Explore." In *Off to a Good Start: Launching the School Year,* 37–43. Turners Falls, Mass.: Northeast Foundation for Children, 1997.

Academic Choice

Children learn best when they are given choices about what they're learning and plenty of opportunities to explore, to make decisions, to take risks, and to make mistakes. One way to give children more choice in their learning and to allow them to work at their own pace and level of ability is through a structure called academic choice, in which children choose their learning activity within a range of choices structured by the teacher.

Teachers have found many ways to structure academic choice. Some teachers structure choices within a particular content area or topic so that everyone shares the same general focus. For example, every child might be participating in a math activity with the common goal of practicing the computation, measurement, and problem-solving skills that have been the focus of study for the past month. There are many choices available for achieving this goal: playing games that use these math skills; creating word problems for classmates to solve; activities such as sewing and building that require measuring.

Another approach is to offer choices within a wide range of content areas. In any given academic choice period, children might be working concurrently in one of the following areas: art, reading, math, writing, science, independent projects, or blocks (K–3). The teacher might structure challenges within these areas, striving for a balance between student- and teacher-initiated activities.

Children reflect frequently, either in writing or verbally, about the work they have done during academic choice, and they have the opportunity to share their efforts and learning with the whole group, giving added meaning and depth to the learning that occurs during academic choice.

Further Reading

- Denton, Paula. "Choice in the Middle Grades: Keeping Play Alive." *Pathways*. Bethesda, MD: (May 1994): 8–12.

Hopes and Dreams: The Starting Point for Establishing Rules with Students

Enlisting children in the process of generating rules is an essential part of the work of the first six weeks of school. Children are more apt to understand and respect rules they help make, and it's important that everyone has a voice and say in the construction of what it means to be a safe, caring, and respectful community.

This approach begins with students and teachers articulating their hopes and dreams for the school year. Teachers provide children with positive guidelines and a vision of a classroom in which care, respect, and responsibility matter. The children's individual hopes and dreams are then incorporated into this vision, and the classroom rules grow directly from the children's hopes and dreams. Through this process, children come to understand and appreciate rules as a social necessity, a necessity that protects their classroom community and makes their hopes and dreams possible.

The process of communicating hopes and dreams, usually begun during the first week of school, serves the following purposes:

- Sets a tone of collaboration and mutual respect
- Builds community and helps children get to know each other
- Invites children to have a say about what they learn in school
- Enables children to understand and feel invested in the classroom rules

The process begins with teachers reflecting on their own goals and dreams for the coming year—what they want most for the children in their classes and what they are looking forward to doing in the school year. "My hope is that this will be a community where everyone feels safe and is able to learn. This year, I have a particular hope that everyone will find something special, perhaps new, to accomplish with pride." In addition to being communicated verbally, children's hopes and dreams are represented visually and/or in writing and displayed prominently in the classroom.

Hopes and Dreams

Modeling

The class moves from articulating their hopes to establishing rules that will help these hopes come true. As ideas are shared and rules are established, the teacher continually revisits the children's hopes to make the connection between individual goals and classroom rules concrete. The teacher's emphasis on the process of creating rules provides a strong reference point throughout the year.

Further Reading

- Clayton, Marlynn K., and Chip Wood. "Rules Grow from Our Hopes and Dreams." In *Off to a Good Start: Launching the School Year,* 16–23. Turners Falls, Mass.: Northeast Foundation for Children, 1997.

Modeling

This is a technique that teachers use when they want to teach a very specific behavior. The teacher models a behavior for the students, demonstrating appropriate actions and language. Students then also model, observe, discuss, and practice the behavior.

Here are some examples of behaviors that might be taught through modeling:

- How to carry chairs in the classroom
- How to show that you are listening
- How to line up at the door
- How to use the drinking fountain

Below is a step-by-step example of how a teacher might use this technique to teach children to pass a friendly handshake around the circle at Morning Meeting.

Step 1: Teacher names and presents the desired behavior.

Example: "I want us to pass a friendly handshake. Watch what I do."

Step 2: The teacher demonstrates the desired behavior.

Example: Teacher reaches over and shakes the hand of a student next to her.

Step 3: Teacher asks students to notice and name the elements of the behavior. Teacher elicits the specific actions and expressions that made this a "friendly handshake."

Example: "What did you notice that made this a 'friendly handshake'?"
"You looked at Sean."
"You smiled."
"You turned your body so it was facing Sean."
"You took his hand."
"You said his name."
"What else did you notice about my handshake?"
"You shook his hand but not so hard."

Step 4: The teacher focuses on "tricky" parts.

Example: The teacher might now focus more attention on the handshake since it's critical in this greeting that the physical contact be safe and positive. The teacher would repeat steps 1 through 3 focusing on the handshake. "I want to be sure I give Sean a firm and gentle handshake. Watch me."
"What made it firm?"
"What made it gentle?"

Step 5: Students practice "tricky" parts by demonstrating and noticing what works.

Example: The teacher asks for students to demonstrate: "Who thinks they can give a firm and gentle handshake?" The teacher then asks the children watching questions like, "What did you notice about the handshake Emily gave Becky?"

Step 6: Students practice behaviors as a whole class.

Example: Teacher says, "Let's greet each other by sending a friendly handshake around the circle."

Step 7: Teacher reinforces observed positive behaviors. This occurs both immediately following the modeling and at other points when desired behaviors are seen.

Example: "I saw people really look at each other. I heard names. I saw firm and gentle handshakes."

Step 8: Teacher continues to reinforce, remind, and redirect as needed. In addition to modeling desired behaviors, the teacher may at times want to playfully model "undesired" behaviors.

Example: The teacher takes hold of a student's hand by two fingers and asks, "Is this a firm handshake? Why not? Show me, what should I do to make this a firm handshake?"

Further Reading

Modeling

Role-playing

- Charney, Ruth S. *Teaching Children to Care: Classroom Management for Ethical and Academic Growth, K–8,* rev. ed. Turners Falls, Mass.: Northeast Foundation for Children, 2002.

Role-playing

Similar to modeling, role-playing is a dramatization technique that teachers use to help children "see" and think about social situations and appropriate ways of behaving within these situations. Role-playing is different from modeling in that it asks for more input from the children and there is not one specific "right" behavior to be taught.

The topics for role-plays come from common classroom occurrences and might include situations such as how to share materials; how to handle accidents; what to do if you see someone making fun of someone else; or what to do when you want to join in a game but no one has invited you. Role-playing helps children to think about the application of classroom rules, to see a situation from various perspectives, and to solve problems. Although the problem being role-played is a familiar one, the fact that it is fictionalized safely removes it from the actual occurrence and helps children to approach it with objectivity.

The teacher begins a role-play by describing a common problem situation, such as two children wanting to use the same materials or a child coming to class without his/her homework completed. The teacher asks students for their ideas about what the child(ren) could do in this situation that would be in keeping with the classroom rules.

For example, the teacher might say, "Pretend my homework isn't ready. The rules say to be honest; the rules also say to do your best work and be prepared for class. What might I do?" The students share their ideas about what the student could do in this situation, and the teacher chooses one of the ideas to act out. For this initial role-play the teacher is the primary actor, although she/he may need students to assist.

The role-play is followed by discussion in which the teacher asks students to share what they noticed about the character's actions, gestures, feelings, and words. Noticing and recognizing the possible feelings of each party involved helps children to develop insights and empathy. The goal in this stage is to help children understand and be able to recognize themselves in these situations without fear of judgment or criticism. In this stage, the teacher might ask questions such as the following:

"What do you notice about the characters' actions?"

"How do their actions fit with our rules?"

"How might a character be feeling?"

"What are some alternatives for how this situation could be handled?"

The teacher then chooses student volunteers to role-play one or two more of the students' suggestions. The teacher concludes the role-play by summarizing the constructive ways of handling this situation which the students have generated and encouraging students to practice the ideas in daily classroom life.

Role-plays are generally done with the whole class, but they can also be useful in small groups or even when working with a child individually. They are most successful when they are kept short (thirty minutes or less) and lively.

Further Reading

- Charney, Ruth S. *Teaching Children to Care: Management in the Responsive Classroom.* Turners Falls, Mass.: Northeast Foundation for Children, 1985.

Logical Consequences

The use of logical consequences is a discipline technique used in many classrooms. It is a way of responding to misbehavior that is respectful of children and helps them take responsibility for their actions. Unlike punishment, which relies on the use of external control, the primary goal of logical consequences is to help children develop inner control by looking closely at their own behavior and learning from their mistakes. The consequences of a child's misbehavior flow logically from what the child did. For example, cleaning up graffiti on the bathroom walls is a "logical consequence" for the child who drew the graffiti; being suspended from school is not.

Three criteria, referred to as the three R's by Jane Nelsen in her book *Positive Discipline* (Nelsen 1996, 86), are used to ensure that a response is truly a logical consequence rather than a punishment. If any of the three R's is missing, the response is not a logical consequence. Logical consequences are:

Related

The consequence is directly related to the child's behavior. Leaving the group is directly related to being disruptive to the group; missing recess is not.

Logical Consequences

Respectful

Logical consequences are respectful of the student and the classroom. Being respectful entails giving students input into possible consequences and including some choices about the specifics of the consequences. Logical consequences are not intended to humiliate or hurt. The same consequence could be respectful in one situation and demeaning in another. For example, mopping the floor during recess is a respectful consequence for the child who chooses to have a water fight at the drinking fountain, but not for the child who fails to complete his work.

Reasonable

Logical consequences should help children fix their mistakes and know what to do next time, not make them feel bad. A reasonable consequence for a child who knocks over a classmate's building would be to help that child rebuild it, not to be banned from block building for the next month.

Most logical consequences will fall into one of three categories:

Making reparations: "You break it—you fix it."

Reparations give children the opportunity to face and fix their mistakes. If a child spills a drink, the child cleans up the mess. The child who accidentally tears another child's drawing helps that child to tape it back together.

Mishandling responsibility—more limits set

When students show that they aren't ready to handle the level of responsibility a situation demands, it is a logical consequence that we restructure the situation at least temporarily, taking back more control, until it is time for the children to try again. For example, the child who leaves computer disks scattered around the floor is temporarily allowed to use the center only with supervision, or the art area is closed for a few days because the class has not been taking care of the materials there.

Time-out

Time away from the group is used when a child is not able to cooperate and is being disruptive to the group. The teacher separates the child from the activity temporarily until the child is ready to participate in a positive way. In younger elementary grades, there is often a designated area in the classroom where children go for a brief time to regain their controls. In older elementary classrooms, students often have input into deciding where their time-out place will be. To be a logical consequence and not a punishment, time-out must be used in a matter-of-fact and respectful manner. The teacher's tone and intent is a critical factor in this distinction.

Further Reading

- Charney, Ruth S. *Teaching Children to Care: Classroom Management for Ethical and Academic Growth, K–8,* rev. ed. Turners Falls, Mass.: Northeast Foundation for Children, 2002.
- Gootman, Marilyn E. *The Caring Teacher's Guide to Discipline: Helping Young Students Learn Self-Control, Responsibility, and Respect.* Thousand Oaks, Calif.: Corwin Press, Inc., 1997.
- Mackenzie, Robert J. *Setting Limits in the Classroom.* Rocklin, Calif.: Prima Publishing, 1996.
- Nelsen, Jane. *Positive Discipline.* Revised edition. New York: Ballantine Books, 1996.

Quiet Time

In the daily lesson plans that follow in this book, there is time allotted—generally fifteen to thirty minutes—in each school day for quiet time. Quiet time helps create an atmosphere of calm, safety, reflection, and restoration. We advocate for a mid-day schedule that includes recess, lunch, and quiet time, in that order. In the middle of the day children need a break from the rigors of academics and the demands of social interaction, a break which will help them to be more productive and engaged in the afternoon.

During quiet time, the rule in most classrooms is that children must work completely alone in their own space and the room must be silent. Children might be drawing, writing, working on the computer, resting, or doing an assignment. In the silence they are often consolidating their learning and reflecting on their morning. It is a reflective and restorative time for teachers also.

Further Reading

- Wood, Chip. *Time to Teach, Time to Learn: Changing the Pace of School.* Turners Falls: Mass.: Northeast Foundation for Children, 1999.

FEBRUARY
MARCH
News and Announcements
Zora is first
Erika is the door holder
Danny and Maria are the
lunch inviters

Week One

CHAPTER ONE

From the moment students arrive at school I try to give them "instant ownership of their room." They need right away to feel known and liked by their teacher. They need to make an impact on the environment, to see that the fact that they are there makes a difference. The children also need to feel comfortable within that environment. The focus of the first week of school is upon getting to know each other and the routines and layout of the school.

DEBORAH PORTER, *first-grade teacher*

Deborah is speaking about first-graders, but her statements ring true for learners of all ages. In the first week of school, teachers must provide plenty of safe, comfortable ways for class members to get to know each other, to share their ideas and interests, and to feel a sense of safety and comfort in their classroom. This requires careful planning and direction of nearly every moment of the first few days.

During the first week of school, when we are getting to know each other and learning basic procedures (such as lining up and lunch routines), there are no general class rules. Those rules will be generated and articulated by the group later. It is critical, however, that children have a clear understanding of our expectations and boundaries from the moment they enter the classroom.

Paula remembers well her son's first day of kindergarten. As they drove home at the end of the day, she asked him how he liked school. He burst into tears. "I don't know what the rules are!" he sobbed. His teacher's expectations were not clear to him. He was afraid he would discover the rules only by breaking them and "getting in trouble." The start to his school career was filled with anxiety!

In contrast, we want children, from the first day of school, to feel secure and successful because they know the rules of the culture. Teaching proactively is essential during these early days. Teachers must discuss and model new routines and experiences and let students practice them before they are actually performed.

At this point, rules are very specific and are related to the concrete actions of each activity—"In our meetings, one person speaks at a time," or "When the bell rings, everybody freezes." Behaviors are modeled and practiced, modeled and practiced, over and over in each new situation. A rhythm of practice and learning is established when children learn how to "freeze" at the bell signal, and it continues as they learn to arrange themselves for Morning Meeting, line up to go outside, use the name tag system to go to the bathroom, etc.

Overview

As adults, we often forget how much knowledge and attention it takes for a child to walk quietly in the hall, invite a friend to lunch, choose a book from the library and settle in to read for half an hour, or pack a bag to get ready for dismissal. In the early days of the school year, we need to break down the steps for each classroom procedure. By involving the children in discussion and by modeling what to do in each situation, we alleviate anxieties about *not* knowing and clarify the teacher's expectations.

All of this teaching and practicing must occur in a rich and meaningful context. As you will see in the lesson plans themselves, much of the content of the first week's curriculum focuses upon and grows from the children themselves. Rather than beginning work in textbooks and workbooks right away, students are learning morning greetings, bringing in and studying family photographs, talking about favorite books, and sharing their hopes and dreams for the upcoming year. Through "guided discoveries," students exchange and extend the good ideas and knowledge they have about using school materials and tools such as math manipulatives, crayons, and dictionaries. These activities form the core around which skills are learned and developed. As students reveal their strengths, and generate and share ideas, they become active participants in their learning and assume increasing responsibility in small, incremental steps.

During the first week, all students are doing the same thing at the same time, though students may be in small groups, with partners, or by themselves at times. The teacher is highly focused upon the process of the group and, when not engaged in active instruction, is observing students and giving them frequent feedback.

In her book *Teaching Children to Care,* Ruth Charney writes about the importance of seeing children and letting them know that you see all that happens in the classroom during the early weeks of school: "My chair, my table or desk is where I can see the entire classroom. When I work with a small group, my chair is turned so that I see the room. I often gather the whole group in a circle so that everyone sees everyone else. I walk in the back—not the front—of the line. I see everyone. And everyone knows that I see because I let them know with my comments, over and over." (Charney 1991, 21)

While the open-ended nature of many activities encourages discovery and presents cognitive challenges, we do not give direct instruction in new skills or introduce content that will be highly demanding for many in the group during this time. We want students to begin the year reminded of all they have learned, not overwhelmed by what they do not know.

Week One

Even more importantly, we want to focus our energy and attention on teaching behavior and establishing a tone. Teachers must be free to see—and to let children know that we see with our comments—the carefulness of work, the kindness of interactions, the attention to cleaning up a table. They must be free to notice also when work is not careful, interactions are not kind, and a table is not cleaned—and to demand a higher standard.

These are the teachings of the early weeks of school—not the new hard math concepts or vocabulary lists. New content and skills are certainly important, and we love teaching them, but they will wait. Teaching the skills of cooperation and collaboration and establishing a productive learning climate allows, enriches, and enhances the academic and social learning that comes later.

It is not always easy to restrain ourselves during these early weeks from leaping ahead and unfurling the year's full-blown curriculum which has been incubating in our heads all summer. "Teachers who come to believe in this approach," writes Chip Wood in *Time to Teach, Time to Learn,* "talk about how hard it is to follow it as they watch their colleagues zoom ahead in the curriculum, how much they worry they will never get their children to catch up. But like the tortoise and the hare, slow but sure wins the race." Teachers who devote time during these early weeks to setting goals, generating rules, exploring materials, and building a trustworthy space for learning find that in the end the approach pays off greatly. "In the long run, time is gained and enriched for teachers and students alike. Discipline difficulties are fewer and less time-consuming than in other classrooms where the social expectations were not a clear focus. There is greater understanding of academic expectations and academic outcomes are improved." (Wood 1999, 205)

The first week is a time to help children see their school as a place where they belong and where they know and can meet expectations. They need to feel comfortable and supported, excited and challenged. By the week's end, the classroom walls display students' work; the air holds echoes of their voices offering a hope, venturing an idea about those curved lines on a globe, singing a new song, or laughing at a lunchtime joke. A new community—with a sense of purpose and with rules, routines, and responsibilities that support that purpose—is forming.

Goals for Week One

Though the details of our plans differ with different grade levels (as you will see in the sample lesson plans that follow), the following specific goals for the first week of school pertain to all grade levels:

Goals for Week One

- **Students and teachers will know each other's names.**
- **Students and teachers will be able to name some interests and out-of-school activities or experiences of members of the class.**
- **Students will know the basic expectations for and will successfully perform the following basic routines of the school day with close teacher supervision and reinforcement:**

Arrival	**Lunch**
Transitions	**Signals**
Lining up and moving through halls	**Work-sharing**
	Whole-group meetings
Bathroom procedures	**Quiet time**
Recess	**Cleanup**
Activity/work times	**Dismissal**

- **Students and teachers will name and share their hopes and dreams for the school year.**
- **Students will generate ideas and procedures for using basic tools and materials for reading, math, art, recess, and writing, and will explore their use further in open-ended activity times.**
- **Each child will present her/his work to the group at least two or three times (with exceptions made for very shy children).**
- **Children's art, writing, and personal artifacts will be displayed around the room.**

Day One

8:30 Greet each child at the door

Name tag and label making

Teach freeze signal (bell) by playing "The Freeze Game"

9:00 Morning Meeting

Teach signal for silence (raised hands)

Teacher introduces each child, and child announces favorite color

Singing: "Peanut Butter, Grape Jelly"

Teach morning chart: read together, then write each child's name on the chart as he/she says it

9:30 Teach bathroom procedure

9:45 Snack

10:00 Introduce outside time

Model lining up

Walk boundaries of playground

Teach and play "Octopus"

10:45 Guided discovery: crayons

11:30 Tour of school

Office, library, gym, cafeteria

Play "Cafeteria" (modeling and practicing lunchtime routines)

12:00 Lunch

12:30 Story time (read-aloud)

1:00 Quiet time

1:15 Guided discovery: pencils and paper

2:00 Guided discovery: playground (swings, slides, jungle gym)

2:45 Teach dismissal routines

3:00 Dismissal

Day Two

8:30 Arrival and morning message on chart

8:45 Morning Meeting

Practice silence signal

Introduce Morning Meeting and generate meeting rules

Greeting: teacher greets each child and presents a naming challenge—"Who can name two classmates? Three? Four?"

Singing: "This is a Song (Not Very Long)"

Morning Message: read morning chart together and discuss children's written input

9:15 Outside: play "Octopus"

9:45 Snack

10:00 Guided discovery: pattern blocks

11:00 Teach and practice fire drills

11:30 Outside: playground equipment

12:00 Lunch

12:30 Story time

1:00 Quiet time

1:15 Guided discovery: books (classroom library)/drawing assignment

1:45 Outside: teach "Fish Gobbler"

2:15 Guided discovery: books (classroom library)/drawing assignment

2:45 Closing circle

3:00 Dismissal

Day Three

8:30 Arrival and morning chart

8:45 Morning Meeting

Greeting: each child says her/his name and favorite food, with teacher modeling first

Sharing: teacher shares something from family life

Song: "I'm a Little Piece of Tin"

Morning Message: read morning chart together and discuss children's written input to the chart

9:15 Outside

Introduce "safe tagging"

Play "Octopus" and "Fish Gobbler" with children taking turns as taggers

9:45 Snack

10:00 Math

Introduce math studies with discussion questions such as, "What are numbers for?" and "What do mathematicians do?"

Read a counting picture book

Sing an active counting song, such as "This Old Man"

10:40 Guided discovery: scissors

11:30 Outside: introduce sandbox play on the playground

12:00 Lunch: assign seats

12:30 Story time

1:00 Quiet time

1:15 Begin work on "hopes and dreams": model, discuss, then draw a picture of an important hope for school this year

2:00 Introduce activity time and assign each child to one of three activities: pattern blocks, crayons, or independent project (scissors and paste)

2:45 Closing circle

3:00 Dismissal

Sample Schedule

Week One

Primary Grades (K–2)

Day Four

8:30 Arrival and morning chart

8:45 Morning Meeting

Greeting: teach simple greeting and practice around the circle

Sharing: specialist teacher shares something from her family or personal life

Song: review songs learned so far

Morning Message

9:15 Outside

"Fish Gobbler"

"Category Tag"

9:45 Snack

10:00 Math: activities with pattern blocks

10:45 Guided discovery: clay

11:30 Outside: playground activities

12:00 Lunch: assign lunch partners

12:30 Story time

1:00 Quiet time

1:15 Hopes and dreams drawings: complete drawings, help children write captions, mount drawings

2:00 Activity time (add clay to activities)

2:45 Closing circle

3:00 Dismissal

Day Five

8:30 Arrival and morning chart

8:45 Morning Meeting

Greeting: repeat simple greeting around the circle as practiced on Day Four

Sharing: another specialist teacher will share something about himself/herself

Song: "Apples and Bananas" or "Sandwiches"

Morning Message

9:15 Outside: "Captain's Coming"

9:45 Snack

10:00 Math: pattern block activities

10:45 Activity time

11:30 Outside: playground activities

12:00 Lunch

12:30 Story time

1:00 Quiet time

1:15 School tour: classrooms

1:45 Model work-sharing, and students share hopes and dreams

2:15 Fire drill practice with entire school

2:30 Outside: "Category Tag"

2:45 Closing circle

3:00 Dismissal

Week One

PRIMARY GRADES (K-2)

Community Building and Tone Setting

First greetings

At the Greenfield Center School, the former K–8 laboratory school for Northeast Foundation for Children, the value the community places upon warmth and welcome is evident even before children enter their classrooms. On the first day of school, kindergarten and first-grade children are greeted outside the front door by fifth- or sixth-graders who introduce themselves and then escort the younger child (often along with a parent) to the proper classroom. Over the next few days, the older children continue to meet the younger ones before school starts and walk them to their room.

Community Building and Tone Setting

This accomplishes many goals. It increases the sense of comfort for the younger child entering this large building full of big kids, unfamiliar teachers, and many rooms. It offers older children an opportunity to practice responsibility and to build connections beyond their own age group. And it helps more reticent children separate from parents and become involved in the activities of the classroom.

Making name tags

As students arrive in the classroom on that first day, I greet them one by one at the door. Children then set to work with crayons making name tags for themselves and labels for coat hooks and storage cubbies. For kindergartners, I prepare the name tags with the students' names printed ahead of time and have them find and decorate the tags.

Ideally, there will be extra teachers available to help the students with this activity, freeing me to greet and roam about, speaking to individuals and helping any child who might be having difficulty with the transition. Specialist teachers such as librarians, special educators, or art and music teachers are usually free and willing to join classrooms for the first fifteen to thirty minutes of the day this first week to help with early morning activities.

As the students work, their anxiety and self-consciousness begin to fall away. Drawing with crayons and writing their names are familiar activities. This is work they can do! In this comfortable atmosphere—with a success-insured task and plenty of adult support—students make reassuring, fledgling connections with other students and with their teachers.

Morning Meeting

Morning Meeting begins right away. Ahead of time, I have assigned seats by placing cards with names on them around the circle. During the first meeting, I introduce each child to the class and ask each child to answer a simple question, such as "What is your favorite color?" or "What is your favorite food?" as I introduce him or her. This is the very beginning stage of the children's learning to share information about themselves with the class, a practice which will become an important component of our daily Morning Meeting.

Week One

Primary Grades (K–2)

"This is my new friend, Maggie," I announce as I stand beside Maggie. "This is my new friend, Alex." The use of the word "friend" is quite intentional and conveys several messages: that the teacher is a friend (albeit a grown-up, in-charge sort of friend); that school is a place to make new friends; and that the teacher expects all classmates to behave in a friendly manner. Although with older students, we would tailor our language to honor their increasingly sophisticated distinctions between friendship and respectful, friendly behavior, this phrasing works well in primary grades.

I might instruct children to respond to each introduction with a group "Hello" or to simply listen and wait their turn to be introduced. After introductions, if time and attention span allow, I ask, "Who thinks they can name two (then three) classmates?"

Next we sing a simple song, "Peanut Butter, Grape Jelly." While the words are available on a large chart, knowing the song is not necessary for participation. I have deliberately chosen a song that is repetitive, easily learned by all, and fun to sing.

The first Morning Meeting ends with the introduction of the morning message chart, a chart that will greet the children each day as they enter the room. Today's morning message contains a heading and two sentences:

Good Morning!
Today is Tuesday,
September 5, 2000.
We will learn names
today.

Sample Morning Message Chart
Primary Grades, Day One

Community Building and Tone Setting

I read the chart, then ask the children to read along with me as I repeat it. Each child says her or his name and I write it on the chart. Later, I will make a more permanent chart of our names to go on the classroom wall. Less than one hour into the school day, each child has been named publicly at least three times.

Subsequent Morning Meetings this week will build from this base. On Day Two, I plan to model how to greet someone by ritually greeting each child myself: "Good Morning, Jesse," "Good Morning, Anna." I tell students that they may return my greeting by saying "Good Morning" back to me, and I let them choose whether or not to do so. This gives me an idea of their readiness to move to the next step in morning greetings.

On Day Three, children speak for themselves. Going around the circle, each child says her/his name and the name of a favorite food. They are learning to speak to the group and to share information about themselves.

Assuming most children demonstrate a reasonable comfort level with these first greeting activities, I teach them a simple greeting on Day Four. I first describe and then model the greeting. "Watch and listen carefully," I instruct.

"Good Morning, Nicole." I speak clearly, looking straight at the sturdy, outgoing child I have deliberately chosen across the circle.

"Good Morning, Ms. D.," she responds cheerfully.

"What did you notice I did with my voice, with my eyes, and with my body?" I ask, and the children share their observations.

"You spoke loud so Nicole could hear you."

"You looked right at her."

"You smiled."

"You said her name."

"You noticed a lot," I say. "Now it's your turn to try."

We practice sending the greeting all around the circle, remembering names and all the details we noticed about how to greet someone. We talk about what to do if you forget someone's name. And for the children who are still uncomfortable speaking in front of the group, I offer to say the greeting with them. I know from experience that this simple greeting will take young children some time to master. We will practice daily until most, if not all, can complete it comfortably and respectfully.

Singing in week one

We continue to sing simple and familiar songs as the activity during Morning Meeting all week. The best songs for these first few weeks are simple and familiar and involve some physical activity: hand motions, sign language, stomping, clapping, etc. Songs that require children to practice vowel sounds double as language arts instruction, as do songs with simple words that can be followed on a large chart.

Morning Message

Morning Message time doubles as reading and writing instruction. Each day this week, the morning chart will begin with the same one or two sentences, followed by a request for children's input. Day Two will ask students to put a check under either *yes* or *no* in response to the question "Do you have a brother or sister?" On Day Three, children are asked to "Draw a picture of something you like to do." Day Four, children choose among three or four options: "How many pets do you have? None, one, two, three or more," and on Day Five, children write or draw something they like about school. By the end of the first week of school, the children have shared a great deal of information about themselves and have had many opportunities to make connections with classmates.

Closing circle

Closing circle begins on Day Two. It is a time for reflection and provides a calm, positive tone at the end of the day. This week, class members gather in a circle at the end of the day, and each one takes a turn to share briefly something he/she liked about the day. Later, the topic for the closing circle might be varied to include something that the class did well today, or something that you could do better tomorrow, or something that you are looking forward to tomorrow, etc. Though the format is simple and the words are few, this sharing requires students to remember and to sort through the happenings of their day, to make a choice, and to communicate with others.

As the weeks go by, I build reflection into the day in many ways. We might gather in a circle for a few minutes after recess or before Friday's science lesson. The questions vary, prodding students to think about different aspects of their learning:

"Say one thing that worked well at recess today."

"Name one thing that didn't work today at recess."

"Think of one thing that made our play practice fun."

"What is something you learned about spiders this week?"

Community Building and Tone Setting

Exploring the School Environment

Reflection is an important tool. As students think together about how their work is progressing, they are actively participating in that learning. As they evaluate and comment, they are building a habit that is key to continuous, lifelong learning. They are learning both from their own reflection and from listening to the contributions of others in the group.

Exploring the School Environment

Outside time in week one

We spend plenty of time outside playing games together and exploring the playground equipment during this first week. This gives children opportunities to build friendships while learning procedures and expectations for working in a group.

Some careful preparation precedes our actual going outside, beginning with a brief discussion in the classroom. I share my ideas about why outdoor play is important in school and solicit students' ideas. I tell the class, "We will spend lots of time this year working and playing outside. Who can think of something we can do outdoors that we can't do in our classroom?"

"We can run."

"We can yell out loud!"

"We can play games that we don't have room for inside."

"We can take our lunches outside and have a picnic."

"We can bounce the balls really high."

"We can climb on the structure."

There is no shortage of ideas, and the list grows quickly. I acknowledge, "Yes, there are lots of fun things we can do together outside. And being able to run and shout and get fresh air helps us think better when we come back inside, too. There are a few things we will need to pay attention to so that our outside time is safe for everyone."

We diagram the boundaries of the playground on chart paper and describe the route we will take on our first trip outdoors, when we will walk the boundaries of the playground together. While still indoors, I show the children how to play a simple game, and I mark where we will play on the chart diagram. I then model procedures for lining up, and the children line up as I watch.

All this preparation ensures that, once outdoors, there is little need for talk and instruction—important, since the children will be excited to be outside and preoccupied with taking in the new surroundings. To add some fun and keep the children's attention as we walk the boundaries of the play area, we make our line into a "snake" or play "Follow the Leader."

Choosing games for week one

During the first week, I choose games that are simple and familiar. Tag games are often a good choice. For the first day or two, especially in the younger primary grades (kindergarten and first grade), I am the only tagger. While I model safe tagging, the children are free to run and concentrate on the rules of the game. By Day Three, we discuss and demonstrate safe tagging procedures before we go out. A few students at a time are taggers in that day's games.

Touring the school

For primary-grade children and especially kindergartners, school can often seem big, complex, and full of large people. A tour of important common areas on the first day helps children feel at home. A trip to the office to meet the school secretary and the principal as they work alleviates anxiety and helps students to know and be known in the building. Other useful places to visit might be the school nurse, the library and librarian, the gym, the custodian's office, and, most particularly that first morning, the cafeteria.

Playing "cafeteria"

I always plan to end the school tour in the cafeteria. Children meet cafeteria workers, watch the teacher (or perhaps a cafeteria worker) model the procedures for getting and eating lunch, and then practice the procedures themselves. We call this "playing cafeteria" because we do not really eat at this time. However, when it is time for real lunch and there are lots of other kids and grown-ups around, the children will be confident that they know what to do.

To alleviate anxiety and competition over where to sit and with whom, as well as to minimize misbehaviors, I assign lunch seats to the children for the first few days of school. This practice allows classmates to sit next to a wider range of peers than they might otherwise choose. As they compare lunches and chat, they establish the groundwork for new friendships.

Rules and Routines

Basic signals

Early in the first morning, I introduce two signals for getting the children's attention—the hands-up signal and the bell signal (this refers to a small bell or chime within the classroom, not the school-wide bell that is used in some schools to indicate various schedule change times throughout the day). While I introduce these signals with an upbeat, playful tone, I also convey that they are very important, to be taken seriously and obeyed immediately.

First, I demonstrate how the bell signal works. I strike the chime and tell the children, "When you hear this sound, you must stop whatever you are doing and look at me. This is called freezing. When I am done speaking, I will say 'melt' and you can return to what you were doing." Later in the year, children will be allowed to use the bell signal to get the attention of the class to make an announcement. For now, it is reserved for the grown-ups in the room. At the beginning of the year, I ring the bell from the same spot in the room each time, making it easy for students to know where to look.

Next, we practice this in a fun way by playing "The Freeze Game." The children mill about and talk. I ring the bell and see how quickly they can hold their bodies still (freeze) and look at me. I count slowly to measure the time. Once they have all frozen, I give them a simple instruction, such as "Touch your nose," and then say, "You may melt." We play "The Freeze Game" often this week, whenever there is a bit of time and the group could use a stretch. The goal is for the entire group to freeze more and more quickly, and to learn to listen carefully to the teacher's instructions once they are still.

I teach the hand signal for attention in a similar way. Once I raise my hand, children are to stop talking and raise their hands as well. This visual cue gets the message to the entire group quickly and quietly.

Bathroom visits

Early on the first day, young students, and especially the kindergartners, need to learn where the bathrooms are and what the routines are for using them. We take a little "field trip" to them, letting the boys see what's in the girls' room, and letting the girls see what's in the boys' room. The less mystery here, the better!

I model the procedure we will use for leaving the room to go to the bathroom—placing my name tag on the bathroom hook, going directly to and from the bathroom, and remembering to take my name tag down when I return. I anticipate that questions will arise, such as "What if you have to go to the bathroom and someone's name tag is already on the hook?"

I want children to understand the significance of the steps in this procedure, so I will ask, "Why is it important that you put your name tag on the hook when you leave the room?" We will talk about safety. "It is my job," I tell them, "to make sure I know where you are and that you are safe at all times. When you put your tag on the bathroom hook, I know that you are in the bathroom."

Meeting rules

Meeting rules need to be established quickly, since our class will frequently come together in whole-group circles. Once children have experienced a Morning Meeting (on Day One), we create rules for it (on Day Two). These rules are very specific to meeting times and are different from broader class rules, which we will establish in the second week.

To create meeting rules together, we begin with a question that, in an age-appropriate way, prompts students to think about the purposes of meetings: "What do people do at meetings?" Or, more specifically, "What did we do at our meeting yesterday?"

"We learned people's names."

"You told us what we were going to do next in the day."

"I got to sit with my friends."

"We sat on the floor."

"We sang a song."

Students will provide a range of answers, generating a list that includes both the concrete details and the broader concepts about meetings. I will add any important meeting goals which they have missed.

I then ask, "If we are going to accomplish these things at our meetings, how will we need to act? What rules will we need?" This approach reflects our view of rules as a social necessity, guidelines that help us achieve our purposes. They are not some whimsical, arbitrary list manufactured and imposed by the teacher.

I guide the children to rephrase negatively stated rules as positive statements and to articulate specific behaviors. "Don't interrupt a person," offers Kate. "Yes," I nod. "Does 'Wait until a person finishes speaking' cover what you mean?"

From many suggestions, a few basic rules will emerge. I will neatly print these meeting rules on a poster and display it prominently in our meeting area (see samples below). A final set of meeting rules might include:

Rules and Routines

- Look at the person who is talking.
- Keep hands and feet to yourself.
- One person speaks at a time.
- Raise your hand to speak.

Samples of Morning Meeting Rules

The rules on the left were generated by fifth and sixth graders, the rules on the right by first graders.

Hopes and Dreams

Introductory discussion

Work on "hopes and dreams" starts on Day Three with a discussion of things we are looking forward to in school this year. I begin by sharing something I am excited about this year.

"This summer I went to school and learned some new ideas about ways to teach reading. I'm looking forward to using some of those new ideas during our reading groups." While the children watch, I draw a simple sketch of myself seated, holding a large book with pages facing outward.

Next we brainstorm a list of the many different things we might do in school. The list is rich with the children's ideas: doing math, making new friends, learning to jump rope, reading books with chapters, building with Legos®, doing lots of art projects. Then each child chooses one thing she/he is looking forward to and draws a picture of what that might look like.

Eventually we will mount these drawings on construction paper with captions written beneath the drawing telling what the picture shows. The mounting and writing session is another time when support staff and specialists could be very helpful, especially with the youngest students.

Sharing our hopes and dreams

The hopes and dreams project provides the topic for the class's first formal work-sharing, a time when the class comes together for the purpose of students' sharing their work with one another. Before beginning the meeting, I explain the procedures and review meeting rules about speaking clearly and listening attentively. I model holding up my drawing and reading the caption beneath it, asking the children to notice what I did.

After they have noted details, such as the way I turned a bit so that even the people on either side of me could see my drawing and how I spoke "in a big, 'meeting' voice," the children take turns showing their drawings to the group and reading the captions. The drawings are then displayed in the classroom.

Guided Discoveries

Basic materials

Much of the curriculum this week comes in the form of guided discoveries of familiar classroom materials (see Key Terms for a description and detailed example of a guided discovery). The guided discoveries generate interest and creativity, establish a shared classroom vocabulary, and teach children how to care for materials.

I might begin with crayons during the morning of Day One. In the afternoon, we might explore the most standard of classroom supplies, such as pencils and paper. This is a good time to model appropriate pencil grip and use of the pencil sharpener as well, if it does not occur naturally in the course of the guided discovery.

Other guided discoveries I might select for this week are books or the classroom library, pattern blocks (which will help us begin math later in the week), scissors, and clay or Plasticine®. I allow a full thirty minutes for the exploratory play phase of each guided discovery. It is important that the children have time to truly explore. This is also a valuable time for children to get to know each other and for me to observe the class. I learn a lot as I watch them work independently with the materials. Sometimes thirty minutes will be more than they can handle well. If the quality of work and interaction deteriorates early, we stop and sing an active song together, do jumping jacks, or play a game.

Sharing guided discovery work

Sharing the work done during guided discoveries takes ten or fifteen minutes. Convening in a circle, each child takes a turn holding up his/her work and offering a brief response to a question I have posed. One day the question might be "What do you like best about your work?" On another day, "What will you name your work?" or "What was the hardest thing about making your creation?" The children practice speaking and listening to each other while they share their good ideas and work.

Activity Time

Activity time begins on Day Three. Children in the class work with a variety of materials, all of which are familiar from previous guided discoveries. I assign a small group to work with crayons, another to work with pattern blocks, and a third to create "independent projects"—constructions of cardboard and various kinds of paper put together with scissors and paste. Activity time prepares the children for future choice times and gives them more practice working independently with classroom materials and with classmates.

I preview a simplified version of the method children will later use to sign up to do an activity or to work in a certain area. As the children watch, I say the name of each activity as I write it on the chart and draw a box beside it (see sample below). As I assign each child to one of the activities on the chart, he or she places a check in the box beside that activity, then goes to the designated area to begin work.

As the children work, I watch and roam about the room, conversing with individuals and coaching behavior. I make sure I notice the positives and reinforce them with my acknowledgment.

"What an interesting way you are using the crayon to outline your drawing."

"I notice the way you are sharing blocks to make that complicated pattern."

"I hear such nice words at the crayon table."

"You are waiting so patiently for your turn with the paste."

I also remind and redirect when I notice not-so-positive behaviors.

"Remind me. How do we carry those pointy scissors safely?"

"If you need the scissors, what can you say other than 'Gimme those'?"

During the final fifteen minutes of activity time, we gather in a circle, presenting and sharing our work in a format like the one outlined earlier in the guided discovery section.

Sample Activity Time Chart

Children place a ✓ in the box next to the activity which they will do.

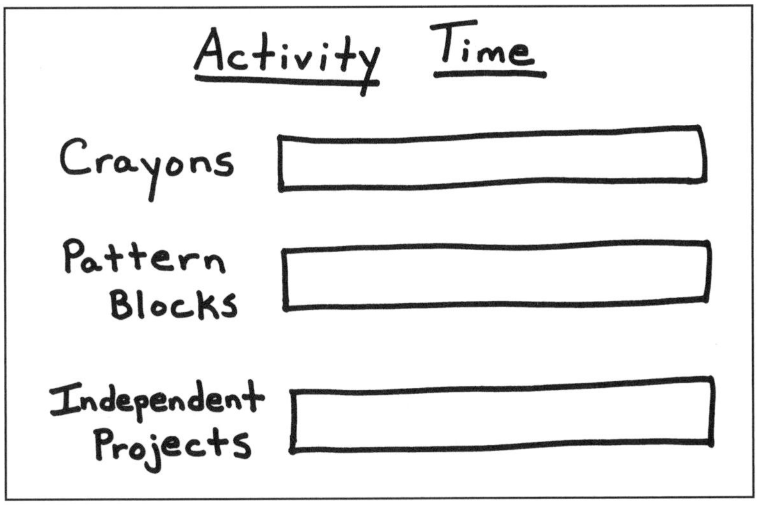

Activity Time

Crayons

Pattern Blocks

Independent Projects

Academics

All academic activities in this first week must be accessible to everyone in the class regardless of skill levels. Specialists often join the class, helping with whatever is going on. They can support special needs students, so that those students are not pulled out of the class during this crucial time for community building and establishment of rules and routines. Specialists are often willing to lead a Morning Meeting, teach a game or song, read a story, or lead an art or outside activity.

Academics

Much of the academic curriculum this week is embedded in the Morning Meetings, games, guided discoveries, activity times, and learning of the routines. Children are learning and practicing speaking and listening skills, sequencing, and following directions. They are reading and learning new vocabulary, writing, counting, and observing. They are developing critical thinking skills and skills of artistic expression as well. As they begin to think about the needs of the group and what rules will be needed to help it function, they are grappling with fundamental concepts of democracy.

In addition to the ways mentioned above, the academic curriculum is embedded this week in quiet time and story time as well.

Quiet time reading

Beginning reading instruction occurs each day at quiet time. At the beginning of the fifteen-minute session, I give each child a quiet time folder containing a book or two, paper and a few crayons or pencils. At first, fifteen minutes of silence is quite a challenge for younger primary children, and I spend much of my attention coaching their behavior to the standards to which I want them to adhere.

I assign each child a place on the rug, on a cushion, or at a table—places separate enough from each other to encourage independent concentration. Once children are settled, I do not allow talking or requests for help from a teacher unless it's an emergency! This frees me to sit with individuals and learn about their reading interests and abilities. As quiet time becomes well established, I can engage in more formal reading assessments with individuals during this time.

Younger primary children are expected to read or look at the books for the first five minutes of quiet time; then they may continue to read or may choose to draw for the last ten minutes. Gradually, the time children are required to read or look at books will increase, although the time might vary, depending upon an individual's reading comfort and maturity.

Story time reading

Story time builds vocabulary and reading comprehension skills. As I read aloud, I stop often and ask the children for predictions, summaries, and opinions about characters and the decisions the characters make. We might discuss the setting and the difference it makes to the story. We might look at illustrations for clues about how a character is feeling or for details that tell about the character's family or where she/he lives. Sometimes I pose a question and list children's ideas on chart paper.

Day One

8:15 Class scavenger hunt

8:40 Teach transitions

9:00 Morning Meeting

Play "Memory Name Game"

Share results of the scavenger hunt

Discuss and model bathroom procedure

9:30 Teach lining up and walking through the halls

9:45 Outside

Teach circling up

Play tag games

10:15 Guided discovery: classroom library

Introduction and participatory modeling

Choosing books and silent reading

Group sharing: children share why they chose their book

11:20 Outside: play "Ship"

11:50 Teach lunch routines

12:00 Lunch

12:30 Read-aloud: *Rikki Tikki Tavi*

1:00 Guided discovery: art supplies

Introduce crayons, markers, and colored pencils

Participatory modeling

Open-ended drawing time

1:45 Cleanup: introduce cleanup jobs and procedures

2:20 Teach format for work-sharing, and a few volunteers present their drawings

3:00 Dismissal

Homework: Bring in a "souvenir" (artifact, map, drawing, postcard, etc.) that represents something fun you did this summer.

Day Two

8:15 Label making: children will use art supplies to make beautiful labels for their cubbies and coat hooks and various areas in the room (art area, library, etc.)

8:40 Practice "freezing" at bell signal and coming to Morning Meeting

8:45 Morning Meeting

Teach simple greeting

Work-sharing: a few students present summer souvenirs

Morning Message

9:15 Outside: play "Capture the Flag"

9:45 Guided discovery: writing

Discuss reasons people write and generate a list of possible genres and topics for writing in our class

Participatory modeling of procedures for writing time

Students pair-share ideas for writing and check in with teacher to report what they've decided to write today

Twenty-minute writing time practicing procedures modeled

Brief work-sharing

10:45 Silent reading

11:15 Reading reflection: "Tell one thing that you read about today"

11:30 Outside: play "Ship" and tag games

12:00 Lunch

12:30 Read-aloud

1:00 Hopes and dreams

Discussion and introduction of worksheet

Individual work on worksheet

Pair-share completed worksheets

2:00 Guided discovery: math manipulatives (multilink cubes, pattern blocks, Cuisenaire® rods)

2:45 Cleanup

3:00 Dismissal

Day Three

8:15 Morning chart: write about one interesting aspect of the day ahead and give children some riddles to solve about classmates (for example, "Who spent the summer in Florida with her grandmother?" or "Who says pizza is their favorite food?")

8:30 Morning Meeting

Simple greeting from Day Two

Summer souvenir sharing (five or so students)

Morning Message: read and discuss morning chart

9:00 Guided discovery: playground

10:00 Reading

Introduce reading logs (model how to use them and create some possible entries together)

Silent reading time with each student making his/her first log entry

Share a few of them, if time

11:00 Writing

Continue brief open-ended writing projects to practice and reinforce yesterday's guided discovery

Use pair-share and teacher check-ins

11:30 Outside: playground games

12:00 Lunch

12:30 Read-aloud

1:00 Hopes and dreams: lesson on symbols and activity

2:00 Guided discovery: math games (Krypto®, Yahtzee®, Pick-Up Sticks®, Dominoes®)

2:45 Cleanup

3:00 Dismissal

Homework: Choose a favorite personal photograph to bring in and share with classmates.

Day Four

8:15 **Morning chart:** check "homework" and ask any students who forgot it to draw a scene from their lives

8:30 **Morning Meeting**

Same simple greeting

More summer souvenir presentations

Morning Message

9:00 **Writing**

Pair-share photographs (or drawings) brought in as homework

Students write about their photos (rough drafts)

Brief work-sharing

10:00 **Outside:** play "Smaug's Jewels"

10:30 **Reading**

Silent reading

Write in log

Brief work-sharing

11:30 **Outside:** playground games (when going out, debrief on how playground time went yesterday)

12:00 **Lunch**

12:30 **Read-aloud**

1:00 **Introduce math activity time:** choosing and working with math games and manipulatives

Teach sign-up procedure for math choice

Model and practice making a choice, setting up and doing activity, and cleanup

2:00 **Complete and share hopes and dreams symbols**

2:45 **Cleanup**

3:00 **Dismissal**

Day Five

8:15 **Morning chart:** ask for volunteers to make a bulletin board of our hopes and dreams symbols

8:30 **Morning Meeting**

Simple greeting

More summer souvenir presentations (final day)

Morning Message

9:00 **Writing**

Introduce standards and procedures for final drafts

Children write final drafts of their writing about their photograph

Work-sharing

Ask for volunteers to make a bulletin board display of the photos and writing

10:00 **Outside:** play "Capture the Flag"

10:30 **Reading**

Whole-group check-in: What are you enjoying about reading? What is hard about it?

Silent reading (begin individual reading assessments)

Write in reading logs and share a few entries

11:30 **Outside:** playground games

12:00 **Lunch**

12:30 **Read-aloud**

1:00 **Generating classroom rules**

Whole-group introduction relating rules to our hopes and dreams

Brainstorming rules

Restating rules in the positive and categorizing them

1:45 **Math activity time** (begin individual math assessments)

2:30 **Cleanup and introduce Friday closing circle**

3:00 **Dismissal**

Sample Schedule

Week One

Middle Grades (3–4)

Week One

MIDDLE GRADES (3-4)

Community Building and Tone Setting

Class scavenger hunt

Community Building and Tone Setting

As the children enter on the first day, I greet them with a scavenger hunt list and a clipboard. The list begins with a directive such as "Find a person in our room who…" and then lists options such as "has a baby brother," "ate toast for breakfast," or "was born in another state." As I hand the children their lists, I tell them that they may ask and answer only one question per person before moving on to a new person. When they find a person who fits the criteria for one of the items, they ask that person to sign his/her name beside the item. The goal is to find a person who fits each item on the list. (See the sample scavenger hunt on the next page.)

This is a fun activity that gets the children moving about the room, greeting and speaking to everyone in the room at least once. Those who are feeling shy often begin by answering others' questions, and soon become a purposeful part of the hubbub. For those who are outgoing, this activity organizes their energy and directs it toward a wider range of classmates than they might speak to on their own. As each child "hunts," she/he begins to get to know classmates better and becomes more comfortable moving about and speaking in the classroom.

Making labels

As children enter on the second day, I direct them to find a seat at the table with their name tag and to decorate labels which will identify their own cubbies and coat hooks as well as various areas in the room. The carefully lettered and beautifully decorated labels naming Art Supplies, Class Library, and Science Equipment say clearly that this is a place where children live. As they help each other to use the special extra-wide, extra-adhesive tape to affix the labels, they grow familiar with and begin to assume ownership of the room.

Scavenger Hunt

Rules: Ask only one question for each person at a time.

For example, if you ask someone named Jon if he had toast for breakfast, you must ask someone else about one of the items before you can ask Jon another question.

If someone answers a question YES, have him or her sign their name next to the item they answered.

Try to find a different person to sign for each item.

FIND SOMEONE WHO:

1. **had toast for breakfast** ______________________
2. **has a baby in the family** ______________________
3. **went swimming this summer** ______________________
4. **is an only child** ______________________
5. **has 3 or more brothers and sisters** ______________________
6. **was born in another country** ______________________
7. **was born in another state** ______________________
8. **went to a different school last year** ______________________
9. **plays football** ______________________
10. **is wearing new shoes** ______________________
11. **knows how to ice skate** ______________________
12. **loves to draw** ______________________
13. **can jump rope backwards** ______________________
14. **walks to school** ______________________

Week One

Middle Grades (3–4)

Displaying student work

By the end of the week, lively exhibits of students' summer souvenirs, personal photographs and related writing, and the visual symbols of their hopes and dreams for the year ahead will fill our bulletin boards and display shelves.

Students who volunteer for display committees will take charge of mounting student work with care, choosing background colors and paper, and considering what the title of the display should be. Questions will arise about details such as how to spell "souvenir" and whether the photos look best in rows or arranged collage-style. Classmates will begin to draw upon each other's talents: "Here, Ella, you can tell when things look straight. Will you hang this one?" "A.J., will you make those cool letters with shadows like you did on your cubby label?"

Community Building and Tone Setting

Students will spend lots of time perusing these exhibits in the days ahead. They point out their own work and locate the work of their peers. By displaying the collective impact of our individual contributions, each exhibit serves as a visual reminder of the power of community.

Morning Meeting

We begin Morning Meeting on the first day. Going around in the circle, each student says his/her name and favorite food and then tries to name the three preceding people and their favorite foods (for example, "Pizza, Travis; ice cream, Will; and spaghetti, Anna"). It is an easy and nonthreatening beginning sharing—lighthearted but not silly. It allows association of names with faces and is a great rehearsal for the remembering of names, which the next days' Morning Meeting greetings will require.

On the second day, I introduce a very simple greeting and lead a conversation about the process. "Each day we will begin our meeting by greeting each other. Watch me and see how much you can notice about my greeting." I turn to Nate, a few students to my right. "Good Morning, Nate." I speak clearly and smile at Nate. "What did you notice?"

"You turned yourself towards Nate."

"You smiled at him."

"You said the name he likes, not his whole name."

"What about the way I said the words?" I prod.

"You said them clearly."

"And you used a cheerful voice."

We go around the circle, exchanging clear and upbeat "Good Mornings," each child named in a welcoming way. We will repeat the same straightforward greeting for the rest of the week, allowing the focus to be on the naming and the tone.

Summer souvenir sharing

I build a sharing component into Morning Meeting from the first day, though the sharing this week is based on teacher-assigned topics. The first day we will share some of our results from the scavenger hunt just completed. We'll go through the list of items on the scavenger hunt form and have two or three children name whom they found for each item. Then all those to whom that item applies (such as "was born in another state") raise their hands.

Week One

Middle Grades (3–4)

On subsequent days, a few students each day will show the summer souvenir they selected to bring in, telling classmates how it represents a part of their summer. We will discuss, model, and practice clear, audible speaking voices and attentive and caring listening behaviors. While this is more open-ended than Day One's sharing, it is still based upon a tangible object, reducing the anxiety of speaking to the whole class without a "prop." The postcards, seashells, camp-crafted art projects, and interesting rocks provide us with glimpses into safe and preselected aspects of each other's out-of-school lives.

Morning Message chart

Beginning on the second day of school, I prepare a chart with a few sentences about our day and an interactive section that requires students' response. I place the chart prominently inside the classroom door and let students know that it is their responsibility to read the chart before Morning Meeting each day. I move the chart into our circle at Morning Meeting time, when we will refer to it.

The chart message on the second day might read as shown on the next page.

Community Building and Tone Setting

9-6-00

Good Second Morning!

At Morning Meeting the following people will share their summer souvenirs:

__________ __________
__________ __________
__________ __________

We will begin using reading logs and we will also learn some fun new math games.

Can you find answers to the following questions:

- ☐ Who spent a month in Florida with her grandmother this summer?
- ☐ Who says pizza is their favorite food?
- ☐ Who has a two-week-old baby sister?
- ☐ Who went to school in Montana last year?

Sample Morning Message Chart
Middle Grades, Day Two

Reflection and Friday closing circle

We will pause often to reflect upon things we have learned, behaviors that are serving us well, and those that aren't. Questions such as "What made our tag game feel fun and friendly today?" or "What made the 'Four-Square' game fall apart at recess?" serve as quick, frequent check-ins and will become a part of the fabric of our class.

Each Friday, we will have a closing circle, a more formal and lengthier reflection time, ending our week together in a calm and thoughtful way. First, we go around the circle, each person sharing something she/he feels proud of from the week that is ending. Then we share a few moments of silent reflection, during which we each compose a wish. These wishes are not for sharing; they simply end the week with a sense of looking ahead with hope. Students whisper their wishes into their cupped hands, and at a signal from me when I note that all are ready, we uncup our hands, releasing these wishes into the air. This small, simple ceremony acknowledges that students' hopes and wishes are a part of our classroom.

Rules and Routines

Teaching basic signals

Before the first Morning Meeting, students need to learn a few procedures and expectations for getting from a noisy activity to a quiet meeting. I circulate among the students, who are engaged in the scavenger hunt, telling them it's time to stop and "freeze." Slowly the room quiets. At that point I show them the chime which I will use as a signal for quiet attention.

We practice freezing. Making it playful, I announce, "Your job is to move around, talk to the people next to you, and ignore me. When the chime rings, I will start counting. Let's see how quickly you can freeze and show you are listening." After a couple of tries, each one a bit shorter than the last, I pronounce it a great "Day One Time" and write it on the chalkboard with a flourish. We will see how many seconds we can cut by the week's end.

Week One

Middle Grades (3–4)

Transition time

"We will need to get to meetings safely and efficiently," I announce. "Who can define 'efficiently'?"

After hearing a few ideas, I model the way I want students to come to Morning Meeting and ask a few students to model it, too. "What did you notice about the way Jamie came to the meeting area?" I ask.

"He put his paper in his cubby on the way."

"He didn't stop to talk to anyone. He just did it."

"When he bumped into Todd, he said 'Sorry.'"

If moving chairs into a circle is necessary for meeting set-up, I model and ask volunteers to demonstrate ways to make this move quick, calm, and safe. Once the children have noted and practiced the behaviors for a safe and efficient transition, I'll signal that it's time for all of us to come to Morning Meeting. We'll practice two or three times if necessary for it to go smoothly.

I will use this same approach of naming my expectations and eliciting from students exactly what each behavior looks and sounds like to teach lining up, walking though the halls, circling up, and lots of other basic procedures these first days. I keep the process engaging by interspersing the learning and practicing of routines with more spontaneous and active pursuits and by using a playful approach to the learning of routines. Students especially enjoy timing themselves and rating themselves on various scales, for example.

Format for work-sharing

In this first week, I give students a specific prompt to focus their sharing or presenting of their work. "Show us your symbol and tell us what it represents," I might say when students are sharing the symbols of their hopes and dreams. Later in the year, work-sharing will be more open-ended, and the audience will be required to ask questions and make comments about the work. For now, we will focus on developing clear, confident presentation skills and attentive listening habits. At the end of each sharing session, we recognize the sharing by a round of applause for those who shared that day.

Outside Time

Rules and Routines

Outside Time

Circling up

Before we go outside to begin group games, I instruct students that when they get out to the playing area, they are to hold hands and make a circle. I want them to be able to quickly assemble themselves so that I can make sure all are there and give instructions. It is a group management technique that is vital on the playground or on field trips.

The children's first attempt will very likely be clumsy and uneven. Some may be swinging arms vigorously, pulling the circle out of shape; some will not want to hold hands with the person next to them; some will be trying to insinuate themselves into the circle near their best friend. I coach and direct until a circle of attentive children has formed. "A good start, but it took a long time. Let's try again, and this time I will count. Spread out, talk, run around, and when you hear 'Circle up!' let's see how quickly you can do it on your own this time."

Choosing games

For the first week I choose games that are familiar to most children this age. I select games with simple rules, games that get everyone moving but do not highlight individual prowess. Tag games, with their infinite variations, work well. Before we begin tag games, we review and demonstrate "safe tagging," and I remind them of the "tagger's choice" rule used in our school: If the tagger says she tagged you, you've been tagged. No arguing, no putting down. This eliminates the squabbling that stems from tagging disputes, often undermining the fun.

Guided Discoveries

Basic materials

This week we will do many guided discoveries of basic supplies: crayons, markers, and colored pencils; multilink cubes, pattern blocks, and Cuisenaire® rods; math games like Yahtzee®, Dominoes®, and Krypto®.

We will continue to get to know each other as we begin to review, develop, and assess our basic skills. Introducing materials we will use in reading, writing, math, and art allows the children to begin work in a reassuringly successful manner. Listening to each other's ideas and watching each other use these materials expand the children's repertoire of techniques. Guided discoveries also ensure that students understand the expectations for getting and putting away materials.

Teacher observation

As the children work on the open-ended explorations of guided discoveries, I watch closely. I comment to reinforce the positive ways they work together: "You are remembering to make sure all the caps are back on the markers," or "You are waiting your turn for the turquoise marker so politely."

I remind and redirect when I see that they need help to be successful: "Show me, Douglas. How can you throw the dice so that they don't roll off the table?" To an impulsive grabber: "Wait, Liz. If you want to use the green hexagon that Stevie has, how can you ask politely?"

I learn vital information about each child by watching. I learn about their reading abilities, listening skills, independence, spelling, handwriting, vocabulary, written expression, and problem-solving skills. A central goal of the first few weeks of school is to assess the knowledge students bring so that I know where to begin and what to emphasize in the coming year. Guided discoveries are among the best ways to do this.

Guided discovery of a learning process

I will use the guided discovery strategy to explore processes in several academic areas this week: how to choose a book from the classroom library for independent reading; how to choose a topic and begin work during writing time; how to play the math games available during activity time.

For example, I might begin our explorations of writing by asking, "What are some reasons people write?"

"People write to say things to other people they can't just talk to, like letters and e-mails to relatives far away."

"My mom writes me and my dad a note each morning, because she has to go to work at the hospital early."

"Sometimes people write directions about how to fix things. Like somebody wrote the instruction manual that came with my new bike."

"Sometimes people write down stories that happened to them because they don't want to forget them or they want other people to know about what happened."

"Or they make up stories that they think people will be interested in."

"What a good list," I acknowledge, recording each idea on chart paper as we go around the circle. "You have named a lot of reasons people might write and a lot of kinds of writing they do. This year we will do lots of different kinds of writing during writing time." We will continue this conversation by listing different genres we might try—plays, stories, letters, autobiography, and poems—and specific topics to write about.

Guided Discoveries

Hopes and Dreams

"I will expect you to find a place and bring all that you need so that you can write by yourself for twenty minutes today." We will talk about what that looks like—and then what it doesn't look like. They smile in recognition as I model an unprepared student, jumping up and down to get a drink of water, sharpen a pencil, crumple and throw away a sheet of paper.

Some of them will struggle to sit in one place and focus for twenty minutes; others plunge in and could write with pleasure for twice that long. Some produce a few tortured sentence fragments; others are on to page two at the end of the writing time. I watch, noting those whom I will check in with first thing tomorrow.

Hopes and Dreams

Beginning discussion

We begin thinking about our hopes and dreams for the school year after we have had some time to get to know each other and do some things together. The depth and honesty of sharing increases as the children have more of a sense of what school will be like this year, and an initial sense of community has developed.

On the afternoon of Day Two, I begin our discussion by sharing my own hopes for our year together, and by telling a brief story of a child I taught in the past. "I remember Charlie, a student who wanted to feel like a better mathematician. He planned to remind himself when he got a wrong answer that mistakes didn't mean he was stupid; they meant he was learning. By the end of the year, he enjoyed math more and had learned many new skills, like division and two-digit multiplication."

Pair-share

As a class we do some initial brainstorming of what our hopes and dreams might be. I want to engage the children's thinking, but I do not want them to commit to final goals until they have had a chance to reflect more deeply, increasing the quality and usefulness of the goals they choose. Individually, children fill out a worksheet to guide their thinking, then share it with a partner (see sample worksheet on the next page). The partner conversations help children develop their thinking through verbalizing their ideas and listening to the ideas of another.

A lesson on symbols

On Day Three, we continue the process by beginning with a lesson on symbols, a concept I know we will be using in our work with mapping as well as in math and language arts this year. We define the word "symbol" and list some of the symbols we encounter in our daily lives—road signs, logos, no smoking signs.

Next, we brainstorm several ways to symbolize ideas such as "reading," "hard work," and "friendship." Several students share their most important hope for this year, as developed on their worksheet the day before, and possible symbols they might use to represent this hope. Then each child develops a symbol for his/her most important hope and creates a final draft of it on a precut square of drawing paper. Children present these symbols to the class on Day Four. We then organize them into a "patchwork quilt," which gets displayed on the wall.

Creating general rules

As students think about their hopes and dreams for the school year, they build an awareness and knowledge of one another. Our community is growing.

Once we have a firm base of shared experiences and a fledgling but sturdy sense of trust and friendship, I begin the process of creating general rules with the class. I have planned to begin this process on Day Five, but I will do so only if my basic goals for the first week of school have been met.

Hopes and Dreams

My Hopes and Dreams Study Sheet

Name ______________________ **Date** __________

Last year in school my favorite thing to do was __________

____.

The hardest thing for me about school last year was _____

____.

If I could change anything about what I did last year, I would ______________________________

____

____.

Illustration

This year I am really looking forward to ______________

____.

I am a little worried about ______________________

____

____.

Our first meeting about rules begins with reviewing our individual hopes and goals. "If these are our hopes and our dreams, what do you suppose are the rules we will need in our classroom to help us make these hopes and dreams come true?" First ideas are often expressed in the negative: "Don't fight. Don't interrupt." After listing these, I help students to express these ideas positively: "So, if we aren't going to fight, what will we do when we have a conflict?"

We end this first meeting by starting to categorize the items on what is often a lengthy list, ranging from grand concepts ("People should be nice to each other") to smaller details ("Talk in a quiet voice during work times"). Our goal is eventually to have three to six general rules upon which the class agrees.

Homework

I find that third- and fourth-graders are very eager for homework this first week. It gives them a way to share their school day with family and to parade their new, advanced grade level.

I keep the homework simple to assure maximum success for all, and I give assignments that literally connect home lives to school. I do hold the students accountable for their homework, checking as they come in to make sure they have done the assignments. I want them to develop good homework habits from the outset, and to understand that homework is never just busywork but is essential to class participation. See Appendix B for further information on introducing homework during the first six weeks of school.

Day One

8:30 Arrival: "Colored Dot Game"

8:45 Teach bell signal

8:50 Extended name tag making

9:15 Nonverbal birthday line-up

9:30 Pair-share name tags

9:45 Morning Meeting

Pairs introduce partners

Review and demonstrate procedures for going through halls and outside

10:15 Outside

Teach circle-up and freeze signals

Review and demonstrate game boundaries and tagging procedures

Play "Elbow Tag"

10:50 Guided discovery: writing

Exploratory activity: write about a day in your life as a short story, news report, cartoon, memoir, poem, or fantasy

Work-sharing

11:45 Review and demonstrate lunch and bathroom procedures

12:00 Lunch

Assign groups of four or five to eat lunch together

Lunchtime challenge: find ten things everyone in your group has in common

12:30 Lunch sharing

12:40 Read-aloud: *Danny the Champion of the World* by Roald Dahl

1:00 Language arts: guided discovery of classroom library

Exploratory activity: choose three books from library

Skim them to select one book to read

Work-sharing

2:00 Outside: play "Giants, Wizards, Elves"

2:30 Closing circle

2:45 Review and demonstrate dismissal procedure

3:00 Dismissal

Day Two

8:30 Arrival: morning chart will have a place to check off how many brothers and sisters each student has, then instructions to find someone with the same number of brothers and sisters

Pairs work together to make name tags for coat hooks and personal storage cubbies; early finishers make labels for areas in classroom

8:45 Morning Meeting

Play "Popcorn Name Game"

Activity: "Zoom"

Morning Message: discuss morning chart and its daily role in the class

9:15 Social studies: guided discovery of globes

Exploratory activity: small groups explore globes and develop "quizzes" on what they discover to exchange with another small group

10:00 Outside: play "Kick the Can"

10:30 Guided discovery: drawing supplies

Exploratory activity: draw a design

Work-sharing

11:30 Outside: play tag games

12:00 Lunch

Assign small groups to eat together

Assignment: share hobbies and be ready to report back to group on most popular and most unusual hobbies

12:30 Read-aloud

1:00 Language arts: independent reading in library books

1:30 Outside: play "Continuous Kickball"

2:00 Language arts: begin regular writing process

2:30 Introduce room cleanup: students brainstorm a list of jobs and demonstrate procedures

3:00 Dismissal

Day Three

8:30 Arrival: morning chart will direct students to contribute to a list of different categories that subdivide the class into smaller groups

8:45 Morning Meeting

Challenge: "Who can name everyone in our class?"

Review and demonstrate simple daily greeting for Morning Meeting ("Good Morning, _______")

Activity: play "The Cold Wind Blows" (use the categories on chart and new ones)

Morning Message: discuss morning chart and add any new categories offered in previous game

9:15 Social studies

Continue activity with globes

Groups exchange quizzes and work together to find the answers

10:00 Outside: play "Smaug's Jewels"

10:30 Math: guided discovery of three familiar math games (Dominoes®, Yahtzee®, Tangrams®)

Exploratory activity: assign small groups to play the games

Work-sharing

11:30 Outside: play "Continuous Kickball"

12:00 Lunch

Assign small groups using a category from morning chart

Assignment: find out who has pets and be ready to share with group

12:30 Lunch sharing

12:40 Read-aloud

1:00 Language arts: continue independent reading and writing process as established

1:45 Language arts work-sharing

2:10 Introduce daily journals

2:40 Cleanup and closing circle

3:00 Dismissal

Day Four

8:30 Arrival and morning chart with an invitation for each student to write something new she/he learned about world geography from the globes

8:45 Morning Meeting

Greeting: "Good Morning, ______" around the circle

Activity: play "A What?"

Morning Message

9:15 Social studies

Complete globe activity

Use "huddle" format for groups to quiz each other on the globes

10:00 Outside: play "Capture the Flag"

10:30 Hopes and dreams: map-making assignment

11:30 Outside: play "Four Corners"

12:00 Lunch

Assign small groups using a category from yesterday's morning chart

Assignment: work together on "Mad-Libs"

12:30 Lunch sharing

12:40 Read-aloud

1:00 Language arts: continue with independent reading and writing process

2:15 Language arts work-sharing

2:30 Cleanup and daily journal writing

2:50 Closing circle

3:00 Dismissal

Day Five

8:30 Arrival: morning chart asks students to check off their favorite part of the first week from several selections

8:45 Morning Meeting

Greeting: "Good Morning, ______" around the circle

Activity: play "Ra-di-o"

Morning Message

9:15 Establishing hopes and dreams for the coming year

In pairs, share maps made yesterday, and then discuss hopes and dreams for this school year

Whole-group meeting: each student shares one goal for this coming year

10:00 Outside: play "Four Corners"

10:30 Math

Introduce a new game to total five games in all

Assign each small group to play a game it has not yet played

11:15 Math: work-sharing

11:30 Outside: play "Capture the Flag"

12:00 Lunch

Assign small groups to eat together

Assignment: discuss favorite places to go for fun and be ready to report back to class

12:30 Lunch sharing

12:40 Read-aloud

1:00 Language arts

Each student writes a paragraph about his/her most important hope or dream for the coming school year

First drafts are reviewed and final drafts are written

1:45 Language arts sharing: students share their hopes and dreams

2:15 Mount and display hopes and dreams paragraphs

2:30 Cleanup and journal writing

2:50 Closing circle

3:00 Dismissal

Sample Schedule

Week One

Upper Grades (5–6)

Week One

UPPER GRADES (5-6)

Community Building and Tone Setting

Community Building and Tone Setting

Social concerns

In the upper elementary grades, friends and peer culture are so important that the social curriculum requires even more careful attention than it does for the younger grades. Sixth-graders, in particular, will likely enter the classroom that first day in September feeling both anxious and excited. They *might* be preoccupied with thoughts of new math challenges looming or opportunities to read new books, but the odds are low! More likely, they will enter full of social interests and concerns.

"I will see all my friends!" some exult.

"Will I have any friends this year?" others worry.

"Will kids make fun of me?"

"Can I be part of the popular group?"

"Will they laugh when I kick the ball or read out loud?"

Taking the time to plan for highly structured opportunities for students to get to know each other better, have fun together, and openly discuss potential social problems and solutions makes a big difference. It creates a powerful way to channel young adolescents' preoccupation with social goals in positive directions, augmenting rather than derailing learning. A focus on fun and playfulness can also help them let go of self-consciousness and open up to new friends, new ideas, and new information.

Even more so with this age group than with younger children, we want to fill the time and space so that there is no room for negative habits and cliques—old or new—to establish themselves. We maintain an enormous amount of control through proactive instruction, while also creating broad arenas where the children's ideas, reflections, and initiative can emerge.

The Colored Dot Game

I welcome students as they arrive the first morning with a warm greeting, followed by an introduction to the "Colored Dot Game." I tell them that I am going to put an adhesive dot in one of four to six colors on their foreheads. They then have two jobs to complete. First, without speaking, they must locate the storage cubby with their name on it and deposit notebooks and lunches. Then they must locate other classmates who have the same color dot on their forehead, also without speaking.

This is an absorbing exercise, because individuals do not know the color of the dot on their forehead and cannot speak. In order to accomplish the task, the children must mix and mingle with a wide range of classmates. Highly verbal students (often the most socially powerful) must spend more time than usual observing, while quieter children (who are often great observers) sometimes emerge as leaders. The social soup is stirred, and communication is forced into more creative and open modes than the group might otherwise be willing to tolerate. The playful, creative nature of the activity redirects energy from awkward self-consciousness to more relaxed interactions with others. Once people with same-color dots have found each other, we have four to six randomly formed small groups, depending on the size of the class.

Extended name tag making

After introducing the bell signal for attention, I ask the small groups to find seats together at one of several locations already set up with markers and blank name tags. "Extended" name tags are simply larger than the usual name tags and include some information about a person along with her/his name. Today, students draw a symbol or write a word representing something about themselves in each corner of the tag. The four corner categories are as follows:

- Your favorite place on earth
- Someone who taught you something
- A time you remember spending three great days in a row
- Something you love to do

When students finish, I give them another silent challenge. This time, they must line up—again without speaking—according to birthday order. The silent birthday line-up requires some skills similar to those required in the dot activity, and it remixes the group. Children are then paired up based upon their order in the line. These partners then share their name tags with each other, sit together at Morning Meeting, introduce one another to the group, and tell two new things they learned about each other.

Mixing and remixing: forming groups

I continue to mix, match, and remix students in a variety of small groups all week. I do this often for group work during academic times, but, even more importantly, I do it during the highly social, nonacademic times—such as recess and lunch—when students are usually left to their own devices.

Some groups will be created through fun activities such as the "Colored Dot Game" and "Silent Birthday Line-up." Other mixing games planned for the first week are "Elbow Tag," "The Cold Wind Blows," and "Four Corners." Sometimes, when time is very short, I will assign students to groups by having them count off, or I will simply put children together who have not been together very often.

Community Building and Tone Setting

Often this week, groups will be designated by the playful use of categories. For example, I might create pairings or small groups by having students locate others who have the same number of siblings. I will continue to use categories all year long as a way to form "random groups." Other grouping categories might include birthdays in the same season, the direction students take to go home from school, the number of letters in students' first names, etc. Categories should consist of clear, verifiable facts about the children rather than changeable opinions they might hold. Experience has shown that fifth- and sixth-graders asked to sort themselves by favorite color, for example, will develop a sudden attachment to whatever colors their best friends have chosen! The goal of giving students experience working with many different classmates is undermined quickly when this happens.

Involving students in group-making

By the third day, I begin to involve the children in the creation of small groups by asking for their ideas for categories. First, during Morning Meeting, we identify criteria for useful categories for creating the groups. "What are some criteria for categories which will result in groups that mix us up in lots of ways—by gender and by people we know really well with people we don't know so well, for example?" This list usually includes items like "It shouldn't be anything embarrassing to tell" and "It should be something people can see or easily know."

Next, we brainstorm ideas for suitable categories to add to our list. Not all the categories students come up with will be suitable for our purpose, of course, but having the list of criteria allows us to select categories based on their meeting the criteria, not on subjective judgment calls.

From the ideas listed in this session, I make a more permanent chart for the wall, and students can take turns choosing a category for dividing the group when needed. Involving students in the thinking behind my strategic planning for creating groups makes clear to them my belief about the importance of an inclusive community in our room without the dreaded "lecture." Allowing them to have input into the categories we use lets us share power within clear boundaries, encourages investment and commitment to the success of the small-group process, and gives me a lot of help thinking up categories!

Positive lunch and recess times

Grouping by many different categories during the first week provides the children with lots of little pieces of information about one another. The more students know about each other, the more possibilities for connection, conversation, and friendship they have. From the first day, they begin this process of getting to know each other with the extended name tags, and continue as we divide into groups based on common interests and traits. Important opportunities for extending this knowledge of each other occur during lunch and recess.

Lunchtime can be one of the most stressful and negative times of the school day for many children. For students in the early grades, some of the stress is about the actual process of the lunch room, such as where to get silverware and how to sort and hand over their tray contents in the cleanup line. Fifth- and sixth-graders are generally familiar with these processes, and their stress has its origin in the social dynamics of lunchtime.

Observe the anxious faces of children as they hustle to grab a favored spot in the lunch line or peruse the cafeteria for an acceptable place to settle with their lunch tray. Social life, and therefore social learning, takes precedence here. Most teachers will testify to the frequently negative impact on academic time in the afternoon of unstructured social time at lunch and recess. This is not a time to leave fifth- and sixth-graders to their own devices!

Instead, the lunch period provides an excellent opportunity to teach and practice social skills that will carry over positively into the academic times of day. For this first week, I maintain very firm control over whom the children sit with and what they talk about. Even if they will not do so later in the year, right now I insist that they sit with members of their own class.

Lunch assignments

Small groups, formed by the category method, are given an assignment that requires everyone to contribute to discussion and listen to each other. For example, on the first day, the challenge for the lunch group is to find ten things that they have in common.

Two goals are accomplished here. First there is little time for negative and destructive behaviors among classmates to undo the community-building and tone-setting work we've done so far. In addition, through the assignment of discussion topics, students repeatedly practice the skills of making positive, respectful conversation with a variety of classmates. They practice positive verbal interactions and enjoy more and more opportunities to learn about each other and forge new friendships. I cannot require classmates to be friends, but I can require that they sit together and make respectful conversation. New friendships will form naturally over time.

Community Building and Tone Setting

While some children this age may object to having assigned lunch groups and being given lunch discussion topics, many are secretly relieved. The "assignments" are fun, and having the decision about seating made for them allows them to relax with each other. Dealing with any arguments they direct toward me is a small price to pay for the increased bonds developed among many of the children in the face of my "strictness!" This degree of rigidity lasts for only one week. In the second week, I slowly begin to turn responsibility for decisions about where to sit and what to talk about over to the children.

During the first few weeks, I join the children during lunch, observing and helping with the conversation a bit when needed. Though it makes the first weeks arduous for me, I really find that the time and energy invested pays back later in the year. I also work with the staff who supervise the children at lunch, letting them know of my "lunch curriculum" and asking their help in observing and giving me feedback. I organize the children into groups, give them their assignment, and immediately after lunch, I check in to hear how it went and what they learned.

Teaching recess

Recess brings another period of the day in which social concerns and social learning dominate, so I plan and supervise this time very carefully as well. I know of some schools where physical education teachers and recess support staff work on plans with the classroom teacher and supervise this time. It is a wonderful way in which the particular expertise of physical education staff can enrich students' experience.

At my school, we do not have a physical education teacher, so I do it myself. It makes the first weeks of school exhausting, but the rest of the school year is far easier and more productive than if I had not invested the time and energy to "teach recess."

We all play together in the first weeks of recess. And, yes, everyone must play! No one is allowed to sit alone reading a book or to stand in small groups, observing and gossiping about the scene. I really believe that the fresh air and the running and frolicking in which young children take such pleasure serves older children as well. As with the lunch assignments, I consider it part of my job description to be the "heavy," the strict teacher who, in the eyes of some fifth- and sixth-graders, "makes us play."

During recess, I resist the temptation to chat with my colleagues, and I really pay attention to the games, noticing and encouraging the positives I see. When I see negative behaviors—perhaps a child trips and others stampede by rather than checking in to see if she's okay—I stop the game and make sure that they understand how I expect them to behave in such a situation before we resume play.

Emphasizing playfulness

I choose games that will build a sense of playfulness in the group. Playfulness, which breaks down barriers between people, is the primary goal of these activities. None of them requires a great deal of skill to participate successfully. In fact, mistakes can contribute to the fun.

Daily doses of outdoor fun, even silliness, provide an especially powerful group-building tool for the often intense, moody, and critical eleven-year-olds. Laughing together puts things in perspective and builds friendships. The games also keep them very involved and busy—we hope they are too busy to be cliquey, critical, and self-conscious. They are learning and practicing positive recess behavior painlessly and mostly unconsciously.

Beginning Morning Meeting

We begin Morning Meeting on the first day with pairs of students introducing each other based on the information gained from the extended name tag making and sharing. On the second day, we continue to focus upon learning names with the "Popcorn Name Game." On Day Three, we begin greeting each other with a simple "Good Morning, _______" passed around the circle.

Preceding the actual greeting is a conversation about the way we will greet each other. Though many of these children will have done similar greetings for years in school, I want to remind them of the expectation that we will greet each other with warmth and respect. Together we name the behaviors and qualities that accompany a warm, respectful greeting. We continue using the simple "Good Morning" greeting for the rest of the week, allowing us to focus upon the quality and manner of the greeting.

I choose activities for Morning Meeting this first week that will emphasize the group's working together, activities like "Zoom" and "Ra-di-o" which are playful and will not expose particular strengths or weaknesses.

On Day Two, I introduce the morning chart that will greet students as they enter the room each day. On Day Three, we begin the daily ritual of reading and responding to interactive components on the chart before meeting. The morning message and subsequent Morning Message segment of Morning Meeting focus on delivering interesting information about the upcoming day and its events in a predictable format from the moment students enter the room. This week, I design interactive components to add to our information about each other and to give students a warm-up for input into discussions. The morning message might include, "Write one thing you learned about world geography" or "What are some categories we could use to divide the class into groups?"

Community Building and Tone Setting

Closing circle

I introduce another ritualized meeting format this week—closing circle. At the end of each day, we will have a brief closing circle. This consists of a simple go-round of the circled group for a brief response to a question. Most often the question will be something like "What did you like best about today?" or "Name one thing you learned today."

Depending upon the mood and events of the day, though, the question can vary from time to time. I might ask, "What do you hope to do better tomorrow?" or "Name a mistake you made and how you fixed it" or "What is one way you helped a classmate?" During these circles, students may pass the first time around in order to have more time to think. On the second round, those who passed make their contribution so that everyone has participated.

Desk and storage arrangements

A final aspect of community building during this week has to do with the way the room is arranged. I group desks or, if they're available, tables for several children to work together. Because I am continually changing the combinations of children in the groups during these early weeks, I do not assign seats.

Personal belongings are stored in cubbies. Supplies, such as markers, pencils, and writing paper, are centrally located and shared by the class. For now all such supplies brought by the students must either be added to the class supplies or kept at home. I notify parents a couple of weeks before school starts about this policy, so that they understand and buy with that reality in mind.

The discipline of sharing, caring for, and cleaning up community-owned supplies creates important opportunities to grow in responsibility, empathy, and problem-solving. It also diminishes the visible distinctions between those who have a great deal of money to spend on materials and those who have little.

Cleanup

The institution of an end-of-day room cleanup in which everyone has a job is also an important part of the first week of school. I involve children of this age in brainstorming a list of jobs for daily cleanup and in setting the standards for jobs acceptably done.

After we arrive at a list of jobs, I make a chart to be posted. I list jobs in one column and have students make Velcro®-backed name tags that I put next to the jobs. We will rotate jobs weekly, and the Velcro® chart system makes it easy to change assignments and to check responsibilities with a glance.

Student work displays

The room opens with few, if any, displays but quickly fills with the work of students. As each activity, from making name tags to writing about our hopes and dreams, is completed, I ask for a volunteer committee of students to create a display of the work in the room. This, along with student-made labels of areas and supplies, quickly establishes the room as the children's own.

Rules and Routines

Less telling, more showing

As with the younger children, rules at this point are specific and are embedded in the modeling and practice of necessary procedures and routines. The less telling and the more showing of appropriate behaviors, the better. While some fifth- and sixth-grade students are beginning to think abstractly, the concrete modeling of behavior is just as important for them as it is for younger children.

They are equally, if not more, resistant to long explanations, or what they might call lectures, from teachers, for different reasons. Remember that for eleven-year-olds, one of the primary developmental tasks is to question authority! They've heard it all before. What they most want to know now is what their peers think and do. Too much verbiage from the teacher cues subversive giggles and eye contact among students, horseplay, tuned-out boredom, or resistance and perhaps argument on the part of young adolescents.

This doesn't mean we can or should gloss over our expectations for performance of school-day routines. While older elementary students are often quite familiar with expected behaviors and routines, they still need to reestablish shared expectations in the new culture of this year's class and teacher. Teachers vary widely, after all, on how they define "walking quietly in the hall," for example, or "freezing when the bell rings." Even more varied are teachers' degrees of tolerance for variation from established expectations. Children are quite aware of this, and if we don't make our definitions and tolerance levels clear, they will test with their behavior until, through trial and error, they have the information they need. This testing can exact a considerable cost on the morale of both teacher and class.

Rules and Routines

Have students model

While modeling and practice are still important, older elementary students need a slightly different approach than younger children. Rather than first demonstrating myself the expected behavior for a procedure such as lining up or freezing for the bell, then having children imitate me, I introduce routines to fifth- and sixth-graders by having individual students volunteer to show and then tell what to do. At first, I call on volunteers I can expect to demonstrate high standards for behavior.

As the children show and explain their understanding of expectations, I can tweak and refine them to my standards by contributing my own ideas. As children practice the modeled behaviors in the day-to-day life of the classroom, I coach them along with my reinforcement, reminders, and redirection. In this way, they learn my tolerance levels. Self-awareness and consistency on the teacher's part can greatly ease the learning process.

"Who cares?"

I often ask students of this age to explain why a particular behavior matters. "Why," for example, "is it important to freeze when the bell rings?" "Who cares?" "What difference does it make to anyone?"

Because many fifth- and sixth-graders enjoy questioning and debating, I will even play devil's advocate at times. "So what if I go out of the playground boundaries? Aren't they just for the little kids?" We do talk a bit more than I would with younger students, but we have some fun together while they "lecture" me. Meanwhile, students listen to each other and learn, examining the world from a slightly different perspective.

Guided Discoveries

Week One

Upper Grades (5–6)

Review and challenge

Since guided discoveries are based upon eliciting the children's own knowledge, ideas, and modeling rather than just delivering the teacher's, they work very well with fifth- and sixth-graders. I begin a guided discovery by asking for a quick review of what the children already know about an item and its use. "How many years have you used markers? What does your experience tell you is most important to know about them?"

After only a few minutes on this question, I move on to a challenge: "Can you think of some productive things you might do with them or learn from them now that you are older?" "Do you know of a possibility for using them that not everyone in the class might know?" "Can we go around the entire circle of students with each one of you naming a different trait of this object?" Many teachers are surprised at how much older children can enjoy a guided discovery. They are often so full of good ideas that it's hard to cut them off and move to the next phase of the activity! They love to share their expertise, and they love to listen and speak to each other.

Introducing a new tool: globes

In addition to introducing some familiar materials through guided discovery this week, I also introduce at least one less familiar and more grown-up item, such as globes. Globes offer a departure from important but more general-use materials, and launch us into a curriculum study of world geography.

The guided discovery format allows us to jump quickly into meaningful new curricula while maintaining the open-ended nature of tasks, which is essential to the initial weeks of school. Everyone in the class can participate fully at his/her own level, experiencing a sense of contribution and success. The activity also provides more practice working in small groups and getting to know each other in the context of a shared task.

A guided discovery of an unfamiliar and more sophisticated item like a globe requires more "guiding" than that of a more familiar or simple material. After an initial whole-group introduction, I send groups off to work together to see what information interests them on the globe they share, and to create quizzes for another group. Later they will look for answers to other groups' quizzes.

After groups have prepared to respond to each other's quizzes, I use the "huddle" format to insert the fun of competition without putting any individual "on the spot." I pair the groups, and each group in a pair takes turns challenging the other group with one of its questions. The answering group then "huddles," putting their heads together and conferring before an individual offers the answer. The challenging team might hum the theme song from a popular game show for thirty seconds or watch a timer to keep the game moving and heighten the playful atmosphere. "Huddling" allows everyone access to group thinking, insuring the full participation of all group members.

Hopes and Dreams

Take time before beginning

Fifth- and sixth-graders take longer than younger students to develop the sense of safety and trust with classmates and teachers that sharing genuine hopes and dreams requires. Therefore, I do not begin until near the end of the first week, and I begin with a concrete and nonthreatening exercise.

Beginning by mapping

The mapping exercise with which I begin is simple. Students make a map of their previous year's classroom. They then create a key and use symbols to show areas of the old classroom that represent the following:

- Something about school they enjoyed
- Something about school that was hard or unpleasant
- Something that they'd like to work on this year

The exercise reinforces our geography curriculum while it asks children to remember their previous year of school. Telling a classmate about her/his map lets a student share personal information and feelings in a fairly nonthreatening way. Students begin to reflect upon what is most important to them, both positively and negatively, about school.

To conclude this process, students write a paragraph about their most important hope for school this year. This provides an opportunity to integrate some writing instruction, and before they write their final drafts, we review paragraph formation. I ask them to identify actions that they will take to help them accomplish their goal and actions that others can take to help them as well. We all need the support of others to achieve our hopes and dreams.

Helping those who resist

For children this age, as self-consciousness increases and identity questions loom, defensiveness also increases. If they fear the judgment or, worse, the laughter of peers, some children may assert a superficial, unrealistic, and therefore meaningless desire for the school year, such as "I hope I get to play computer games all day." Some may try to make a joke of the whole process by naming a goal of "having the school turn into the mall," or "having recess all day."

Waiting until Day Four of the year to begin working on hopes and dreams avoids much of this behavior. Most students will have decided that it is safe to share their real hopes by then, although a few may still need redirection. I handle the resisters with a combination of a light touch and serious intent.

"Though you might well wish for school to turn into a video arcade, William, it isn't likely to happen—not this year, at least! But I really want school to be a place where all students find some enjoyment and get to work at things that really matter to them. I believe that there are things that are within the realm of possibility that you could name, things that we could help come true. Do you want to think some more on your own, or would you like me to make some suggestions?"

At his invitation, I wonder whether something having to do with our small but growing computer center might appeal to him, an idea William endorses. His final draft expresses that he wants to spend as much time as he can learning as much as he can about computers this year. While not all conversations proceed quite so directly to an enthusiastic investment, I have found that students do welcome the invitation to comment about what matters to them in school when they are assured of a respectful audience.

Week Two

CHAPTER TWO

This week I feel like I'm getting my voice as a teacher. Am I Miss Nelson or Viola Swamp? Am I a nag or someone who chooses to ignore a lot of kid behavior if it doesn't cross the line? Where is the line? Monday I felt like I was in a large, round raft with the kids and there were twenty-one paddles in the water. The challenge was to get into the current where we could move in a good direction together. It felt like we were making progress by the end of the week.

DONNA SKOLNICK, *second-grade teacher, and co-author of* On Their Way,
writing in her journal about the second week of school
(Fraser and Skolnick 1994, 46)

The second week of school is indeed a week when the challenge is to get all members of the class "in the current." To extend Donna Skolnick's metaphor, we have introduced a great deal to our "rowers" in the first week. We have introduced them to each other and school staff, to their day, and to their environment. Now, in the second week, we want to get them out on the river and, slowly and intentionally, begin to turn some of the rowing over to them while still maintaining our constant oversight and monitoring.

In Morning Meeting, for example, we introduce sharing—a format that provides a way for the group to learn about each other and to listen and respond to each other in caring, respectful ways throughout the year. We also introduce the ritual of daily greetings, which requires students to choose whom they will greet rather than simply going around the circle. However, this comes only after a discussion about what we should consider when choosing someone to greet, helping children move beyond popularity and their own personal comfort as reasons to choose someone. Building trust, safety, and a sense of community remains a central goal.

This is the week to complete the rule-making process. In this process, students are challenged to construct a set of broad rules that will help the classroom be a safe and enriching place for all to learn. Along the way, they name and examine many of the specific behaviors practiced in last week's procedures and routines. They are frequently asked questions such as "What made our meeting a place where everyone could speak?" or "What made the tag games fun?" or "Why is it important that we put our chairs up on the tables at the end of the day?" We work to create a vision of our classroom community as supportive of all its members. Specific, concrete actions grow from this vision.

Overview

The discussions during this process help children and teachers think about the needs and responsibilities of the community and the individual. We have listened to first-graders consider how to seat their six-year-old bodies comfortably at meeting, while also allowing enough room for everyone to fit on the rug. We have listened to sixth-graders try to draft language that acknowledges both their need to have special friends and the need for the classroom to be a place where everyone feels included. We have listened to faculty wrestle with questions raised by Awards Ceremonies—trying to invent a process which reconciles the genuine individual need for recognition with the awareness that in a healthy community the worth of every member is noted.

To accept individual and community needs and to strive for a synthesis which accommodates both of them is a heady and lifelong dialectic. Solutions that respect the complexity of issues raised in the classroom are never easy, often imperfect, and occasionally impossible. Yet even when the solutions are flawed, there is extraordinary value and learning in the process. It is a process which encourages autonomy, since acting autonomously requires understanding personal and community needs and behaving in ways that respect both.

In the process of constructing the rules, we often name and discuss relatively abstract and profound ideas, such as care, respect, and effort. By interpreting those ideas in conversations and applying them to common classroom situations, the class examines concrete manifestations of the theoretical.

For example, a teacher might ask, "What does 'care for each other' mean when someone's feelings have been hurt?"

"Say you are sorry," is one child's answer.

"See if there's something you can do to make the person feel better."

Or, "How do we show that we 'respect others' when we are lining up to go outside?"

"Don't cut in line."

"Say 'excuse me' if you bump somebody by accident."

Rather than scheduling separate times to teach children how to follow the rules, we plan activities—from games and group initiatives to math and spelling lessons—which will provide opportunities to apply the rules. Children rehearse, discuss, practice, and reflect on ways to honor the newly articulated rules.

We learn, after all, not just from an experience itself, but from processing it. As fourth-grade teacher and writer Steven Levy says, "Experience is *always* the beginning, but it is also *only* the beginning.... I want to help my students develop a habit of reflection to mine meaning and understanding from whatever experiences they encounter." (Levy 1999, 73)

Week Two

Students rehearse for planned experiences and reflect on them. "How can we make lunch a pleasant time for everyone?" might serve as a warm-up discussion question, and afterward we can check in quickly to see how it went.

The group initiatives for children in the middle and older elementary grades this week require cooperation and group problem-solving for the group to succeed. After many of these group projects, as well as many of the outside games, teachers can provide an opportunity for reflection with questions such as "What did we do that made this game fun?" or "What was hard about playing this game?" or "What could we do to make it better?"

In the second week, we also introduce academic choice times (activity time in younger grades) and launch the first thematic study of the year. We choose the theme for this first unit carefully, selecting a topic that gives children a sense of accomplishment by conquering something unknown, learning new techniques, or using new materials. Our lesson plans and the reflections that follow include some of our thinking in choosing the three themes described: spiders, caves, and explorers.

Some of the formal academic curriculum for the year is initiated this week, taking care that chosen areas and activities still involve primarily open-ended instruction that will be appropriate and engaging for all children. In each subject area, we begin with content that calls upon the children's current knowledge while encouraging them to expand their thinking to the next step. For example, our study of spiders in the primary grades begins with the question "What do you know about spiders?" Later we ask, "What do you want to know about spiders?"

So much can be established in a few, short, all-absorbing days that it may be tempting to jump ahead to the tempo of last June when the classroom functioned at full speed and intensity. But we are regularly reminded that the third-grader who looks so grown up and is so eager for hard math problems still has one new sneaker planted in second grade. Younger students are often dealing with bigger changes. "Mommy, mommy," cries five-year-old Monique, tugging at her teacher's sleeve. "You mean 'teacher,'" corrects Erica matter-of-factly, standing nearby.

"Oops," says Monique.

So much has already happened, so much has been shared. It is easy to forget that it is still early in September—still very much a time of transitions. "Oops" are frequent, and matter-of-fact corrections are necessary. It is only the second week of school.

Overview

Goals for Week Two

The goals, across grade levels, for the second week of school are as follows:

- **The class will work together to formulate and agree upon a set of classroom rules.**
- **Daily academic choice or activity time will be established.**
- **Children will work in small groups as well as individually, in pairs, and in the whole group.**
- **Games and group initiatives, including debriefing and reflection time, will occur regularly.**
- **A few curriculum sequences will begin.**
- **Children will regularly work, play, and socialize in structured, teacher-supervised activities with a range of classmates.**

Goals for Week Two

Day Six

8:30 Arrival and morning chart

8:45 Morning Meeting

Continue with greeting introduced on Day Four

Share around the circle: "something I am good at"

Song from Week One

Morning Message: the chart now contains three ritualized sentences and one varied sentence each day

9:15 Math: continue pattern block activities

10:00 Outside: group game

10:30 Snack

10:45 Rule-making session/ activity time

11:30 Outside

12:00 Lunch

12:30 Story time

12:55 Quiet time

1:15 Guided discovery: games

2:00 Activity time: add games

2:45 Closing circle

3:00 Dismissal

Day Seven

8:30 Arrival and morning chart

8:45 Morning Meeting: introduce sharing

9:15 Math: pattern block activities

10:00 Outside: group game

10:30 Snack

10:45 Rule-making completion and activity

11:30 Outside

12:00 Lunch

12:30 Story time

12:55 Quiet time

1:15 Introduce Science

"What do scientists do?"

Observations

2:00 Activity time

2:45 Closing circle

3:00 Dismissal

Day Eight

8:30 Arrival and morning chart

8:45 Morning Meeting: all four components in place

9:15 Math: guided discovery of multilink cubes

10:00 Outside: group game

10:30 Snack

10:45 Science: observations and presenting

11:30 Outside

12:00 Lunch

12:30 Story time

12:55 Quiet time

1:15 Guided discovery: markers

2:00 Activity time: add markers

2:45 Closing circle

3:00 Dismissal

Sample Schedule

Week Two

Primary Grades (K–2)

Day Nine

8:30 Arrival and morning chart

8:45 Morning Meeting

9:15 Math: multilink cube activities

10:00 Outside: group game

10:30 Snack

10:45 Science: introduce unit topic—spiders

11:30 Outside

12:00 Lunch

12:30 Story time

12:55 Quiet time

1:15 Begin class quilt project

2:00 Activity time

2:45 Closing circle

3:00 Dismissal

Day Ten

8:30 Arrival and morning chart

8:45 Morning Meeting

9:15 Math: multilink cube activities

10:00 Outside: group game

10:30 Snack

10:45 Science: spiders

11:30 Outside

12:00 Lunch

12:30 Story time

12:55 Quiet time

1:15 Quilt project

2:00 Activity time

2:45 Closing circle

3:00 Dismissal

Week Two

PRIMARY GRADES (K-2)

Community Building and Tone Setting

During the second week of school, we continue to focus primarily on inclusive, whole-group activities and games. Seats are still assigned for meetings and activities. Outside games are still structured and led by the teacher.

The message chart

Community Building and Tone Setting

Morning Meeting continues to evolve. This week the morning message chart displays three predictable sentences. In addition to today's date, it will name a student who is "first" (in line) and a student who is "the door holder" each day. These three sentences will remain all year long; with this repetition, even nonreaders will be able to read the chart before long. A final sentence (later in the year, several sentences) will vary each day and contain an interesting piece of information about the day, such as "We will start to make a quilt today," and a question to which children can respond on the chart (see sample chart on the next page). The Morning Message time at Morning Meeting continues to be a time to read the chart together and discuss the children's input on it.

Sharing at Morning Meeting

If students seem to be comfortable with the greeting routine, I introduce sharing this week. I begin by asking students what they remember about the teachers' sharings from last week.

I then ask, "Why do you think we have sharing?" Answers usually center upon the idea of getting to know each other better. Then, "What did the sharers last week do to make their sharing interesting and friendly?" I will model sharing once again, this time directing the children to "watch me and see how I do it." I make sure that they note that I chose a couple of important details about my news, but did not try to share everything, and that I used a strong, clear voice.

After students have named important characteristics of my sharing technique, we brainstorm a list of topics for sharing during Morning Meeting. Unless a suggestion is wildly inappropriate, I do not censor. I want the children to generate a broad list of choices and to feel accepted as they are. If the children seem most comfortable sharing toys at first, I accept that, even though eventually I want to move them toward more verbal reports and discussions of events in their lives. If there is time, I ask for a volunteer to try sharing about a topic from the list.

For the remainder of the week, there will be a space for three new volunteers each day to sign up for sharing on the morning message chart. I use a few moments during the fifteen minutes before meeting to rehearse volunteers' sharing with them. If there are few volunteers, I ask specific children if they would be willing to share.

Responding to sharing

In addition to listening attentively, audience members must respond with thoughtful questions and comments. After my first sharing, I ask the whole

Week Two

Primary Grades (K–2)

Sample Morning Message Chart
Primary Grades, Week Two

Good Day!
Tanya is first.
Rob is the door holder.
Today is Thursday, September 14, 2000.
We will start to make a quilt today.
Do you have a quilt in your home?

Yes	No

group to think of questions they might ask to find out more about my news, or comments they might make to show their interest.

Questions and comments often begin as repetitive and formulaic responses, such as "I like your baseball mitt" or "Could you tell more about your dog?" or "You must have felt ______." I remind myself that I have all year to move the children along to more varied responses. They will also have many opportunities to learn when to reply to a classmate's sharing or question or comment with such phrases as "Thank you," "Congratulations," and "I'm sorry." I will model these phrases, as appropriate, and sometimes bring them to the children's attention with a mini-lesson.

Community Building and Tone Setting

Outside games continue

Outside games are an important means to teach listening and physical skills as well as social skills, and they continue much as they did the first week. If the children are ready for new games, I teach them. If they are meeting the challenges of the games successfully, they are ready for approaches and new games that require a greater degree of cooperation. I might teach "Blob Tag" or "Hospital Tag," or add more complex components to games such as "Fish Gobbler" and "Captain's Coming." If the group finds cooperation difficult, I ease the challenge with games like "Red Light, Green Light" or "Mother, May I?" which require less cooperation among the children to play.

The quilt project

On Day Nine, we begin a quilt project, combining art and handwriting instruction with a very satisfying group-building activity. It is a rudimentary type of collaborative work, with each student contributing an individual piece of work that will be assembled into a whole.

First, students draw, on squares of paper, a picture of something they can do well. They then practice writing their names in their best handwriting. I give each child a square of muslin fabric upon which to draw a "final draft" of his/her picture and name with fabric markers. The process of multiple drafts underscores the importance of planning and of practice, concepts that we will use across the curriculum all year long. Teachers or parent volunteers sew the squares into a quilt that will be hung banner-like in the classroom. The quilt is a visually striking testimony to the power of our collective effort as well as a reminder of individual competencies.

Daily guided discovery and activity times

I will add a few new materials to the room—markers, multilink cubes, and a couple of new games—through guided discoveries this week. As materials that draw upon a range of learning styles and modalities are added, more and more children have a chance to shine and to receive recognition from their classmates. We complete a short unit on pattern block geometry and begin a counting and adding unit based upon activities with multilink cubes.

Guided discovery and activity times also enhance the group's sense of belonging and community. Children participate in developing the routines, appropriate procedures, and vocabulary for all the classroom materials. They share their ideas with each other and learn from each other as they generate ideas with the teacher, participate in exploratory play, and present their work. "What do you mean, *alternate* orange and blue cubes?" Steven asks Rosie as they experiment with the multilink cubes. I continue to get to know the children better, and the children practice applying our newly developed classroom rules to actual situations.

Rules and Routines

Creating a set of class rules

I begin creating a set of class rules with the children on Day Six. Referring to the newly displayed drawings of their hopes and dreams, I ask, "Who can remind us of some of the things people in our class are looking forward to in school?" After a few children have spoken, I remind the class of the way we made our meeting rules last week: "We started by thinking about why we have meetings. These drawings help us think about why we have school. What are some rules we will need to follow if we are all going to be able to enjoy doing the things shown in these drawings?"

Embedded in these few sentences and my question is a solid and nonnegotiable expression of my vision of our classroom. This will be a place where we *will* enjoy doing things that matter to each and every one of us. And we all will have some responsibilities in the group and to the group to make this happen. The specific rules that will be named will differ at various ages and from group to group, and it is important for students to think through and name these specifics. The specifics may be "up for grabs;" the vision is not.

"We shouldn't fight or push," children often respond.

"Do what the teacher says."

"Don't run around and don't wreck things."

I write their ideas on the chart in the form they share them. If they seem to be leaving out important ideas that I want addressed, I add them to the list as my ideas.

Stating the positive

After about ten rules have been suggested, we stop brainstorming and I go through each rule listed. "If we're not going to fight or push each other, what will we do instead when we feel mad?"

"Use words. Say, 'I didn't like that.'"

"Get a teacher to help you if you're mad."

Rules and Routines

Next to the original rules, I write these rules, now stated in the positive. By the time this task is complete, twenty to thirty minutes have passed and the children need a break from sitting. We finish the session with a short activity time.

Categorizing the rules

The following day, I present our list of rules, all stated in the positive, written neatly on a chart. "These are good rules, but there are an awful lot of them," I remark. "It's hard to remember so many rules. Let's see if some of them could go together. What about this rule about using words when we get mad at people? Are there other rules here that are sort of like that one?"

"Listen when people talk."

"Let people play with you if they ask."

I know that all of our rules will inevitably fall into one of three categories: care for others, care for ourselves, and care for our environment. As I guide the children to group the rules, I keep these categories in mind.

Once the rules have been combined into three to five groups, I ask the children, "What do all the rules in this group seem to be about?" In the case of the rules listed above, the children may say that they are about being nice to others—or about treating others the way we want to be treated, if they are familiar with the golden rule.

I will use their ideas to compose one rule that encompasses each category. "So, it seems like a rule that covers all these rules could be 'Be nice to each other' or 'Take care of each other.' Can we agree on one of those?" If need be, we will vote on one of the two final suggestions.

Displaying the rules

The discussion in which we consolidate and categorize the rules on Day Seven takes about twenty minutes. After we have agreed upon a set of three to five class rules, the children draw pictures that illustrate children following one of the rules. By the following day, I will have each rule written on a piece of oak tag and mounted on the wall. The children will post their drawings beneath the rule illustrated.

Opportunities to teach the rules

With the rules established, all activities of the day offer opportunities to teach the children how to follow them. "Our rule says to 'Be Safe.' So how will we need to move when we go from meeting to math activities?"

"Who can show us what that looks like?"

"What did you notice about how Asa showed us how to go to math activities?"

"Now, everyone practice following our rules while we get ready for math. I'll watch."

As the children "practice," I observe carefully and coach their behavior. "I notice that you are really moving quietly!" I exclaim. Or, "Andrew, show me how to carry the pattern blocks safely."

Using role-playing

I note where children are having difficulty following the rules and plan role-plays for those situations. For instance, if I observe children having difficulties sharing pattern blocks during math time, I will plan to begin math time the following day with a role-play about sharing pattern blocks. As I get to know the children better, I will be able to predict some areas of difficulty in advance and include role-plays to deal with those difficulties in the introduction to the activity.

One year, for example, I had a group that was extremely competitive, a trait that was clear from the first day of school. Several dominant children had a strong need to be "best," and they were quick to point out others' shortcomings in their efforts to gain that title. With that group, before introducing the class quilt activity, I initiated a role-play using the situation of a student believing a neighboring student's work was not very good. "What could you say to that person and still follow our rule of being nice to everyone?" I asked. After choosing one of the students' suggestions and using it myself in the role-play, I asked a few children to take turns choosing other suggestions to act out.

Academics

Language arts

The language arts curriculum continues like last week, with much of the instruction and practice happening during Morning Meeting, story time, and quiet time. Quiet time is extended to twenty minutes, with book time now lasting for at least ten minutes of that time.

A room full of print

Academics

The room is filling with environmental print—hopes and dreams, student-illustrated class rules, charts of words to songs and chants, and our list of "what scientists do." New songs and chants for outside games are accompanied by charts of words for the children to read with me in unison, or for volunteers to read specific words on their own. Handwriting is introduced as children are taught to write their own names "beautifully" until they are ready to write them indelibly on the quilt block. A predictable morning message greets the children each day with frequent opportunities to write on the chart. Science observations offer new opportunities for writing as well.

Studying spiders

Science begins with the question "What do scientists do?" followed by the children learning how to make and record careful observations of an object, such as a bone or a particularly interesting rock. Ellen Doris, teacher and author of *Doing What Scientists Do: Children Learn to Investigate Their World,* writes about the importance of teaching the skill of observation: "Over the course of the year, I'll hope to see children involved in all kinds of science activity (collecting, classifying, hypothesizing, experimenting), but initially I emphasize observation.... Observation serves as the springboard for children to engage in work that is far broader in scope than simply looking at an object." (Doris 1991, 51–52)

Once the children have learned and practiced the observation process, we begin work on the first topic—spiders! Spiders make a great first science topic in primary grades. They are startling! Gruesome! Scary! Gross! They are also accessible for direct observations, and since they are seen everywhere, they provide for great school-to-home connections.

Some early sharings at Morning Meeting might very well be of spiders found at home and brought excitedly to school. The study of spiders also gives the class an immediate identity and a certain cachet, as it ignites the interest of not only the primary grade children, but of many children in other classrooms as well. We often get many visitors who want to see our spiders and share information about them. (Of course, in certain parts of the country, studying spiders could be a dangerous venture. Many other topics could work just as well—leaves, butterflies, rocks—as long as the object to be studied is easily accessible and meaningful to the children.)

Brainstorming

Spider study begins with a brainstorming session: "What do we know about spiders?" and "What do we want to know about them?" I list students' ideas on chart paper as they share them.

Week Two

Primary Grades (K–2)

Next, the children observe spiders, fill out observation worksheets, and report back to the group. The spiders will be observed repeatedly over many days, and each time children will learn something new. "Do they all have eight legs?" "Mine has spots. Does yours?" "Hey! Their bodies have two parts to them."

After some direct observation, I start a library shelf with books about spiders, and I read some at story time. We list new facts as we learn them from our observations and our books. A local expert on spiders might visit the group to give a short talk and answer students' questions.

Day Six

8:15 **Arrival and morning message chart:** message to include "Write one rule you remember from our Friday rule-making session"

8:45 **Morning Meeting**

Simple greeting from Week One

Introduce sharing: a simple focused sharing about the children's weekend

Morning Message: review rules children remembered and add ones they forgot

9:15 **Academic choice:** expand the choices available

10:00 **Academic choice:** work-sharing

10:20 **Outside:** group initiative—"Lean-To"

10:50 **Rule-making:** work in small groups to create three to five general rules for our class

11:30 **Outside:** tag games

12:00 **Lunch**

12:30 **Read-aloud**

1:00 **Begin theme work on caves**

2:00 **Math:** begin "Investigations" math curriculum with whole group

2:45 **Cleanup and brief closing circle**

3:00 **Dismissal**

Day Seven

8:15 **Arrival and morning message**

8:30 **Morning Meeting:** introduce sharing with questions and comments, and generate ideas for sharing topics

9:00 **Academic choice time**

10:00 **Outside:** group initiative—group juggling

10:30 **Rule-making:** small groups from yesterday finalize proposals and rehearse for presentation to group

11:00 **Rule-making:** presentation of small-group proposals for rules and class vote on three to five favorite rules

11:30 **Outside:** "Giants, Wizards, Elves"

12:00 **Lunch**

12:30 **Introduce quiet time**

12:50 **Read-aloud**

1:15 **Theme:** teach "chain reaction" format for small groups and use the format to generate questions students have about caves

2:00 **Math:** "Investigations" with whole group

2:45 **Cleanup and brief closing circle**

3:00 **Dismissal**

Day Eight

8:15 **Arrival and morning message:** message asks for volunteers to sign up to make posters of classroom rules

9:00 **Morning Meeting**

Handshake greeting
Sharing
Morning Message

9:30 **Academic choice time**

10:00 **Outside:** group initiative—"Everybody Up"

10:30 **Language arts**

Introduce "priority words" and review first ten on the list

Children read twenty minutes in their independent books, make reading log entries, and underline all of the priority words used in log entries

11:30 **Outside:** playground games

12:00 **Lunch**

12:30 **Quiet time:** reading, writing, drawing choice

12:50 **Read-aloud:** *Caves and Caverns* by Gail Gibbons

1:15 **Theme**

Small groups use "chain reaction" format to list on chart paper what they learned about caves during read-aloud

Bring lists to whole group and share

2:00 **Math:** "Investigations"

2:45 **Cleanup and brief closing circle**

3:00 **Dismissal**

Day Nine

8:15 Arrival and morning chart: review priority words from yesterday

8:30 Morning Meeting

Handshake greeting
Sharing
Morning Message

9:00 Academic choice time

10:00 Outside: group initiative—"Knots"

10:30 Language arts

Introduce next ten priority words

Independent reading and log entries underlining priority words

11:30 Outside: playground games

12:00 Lunch

12:30 Quiet time

12:50 Read-aloud: finish *Caves and Caverns*

1:15 Theme: small groups use "chain reaction" format to list what they learned about caves, then share with whole group

2:00 Math: "Investigations"

2:45 Cleanup and brief closing circle

3:00 Dismissal

Day Ten

8:15 Arrival and morning chart: ask for ideas for meeting rules

8:30 Morning Meeting

"Snap, Clap" greeting
Sharing
Morning Message: generate meeting rules based on class rules and use ideas from morning message

9:00 Academic choice time

10:00 Outside: group initiative—"Inchworm"

10:30 Language arts: introduce final ten priority words and follow format of last two days

11:30 Outside: play kickball

12:00 Lunch

12:30 Quiet time

12:50 Theme topic choice

Brainstorm ways students can use room supplies to show what they learned about caves this week

Proceed with topic choice sequence (choice sign-up, planning, working, work-sharing)

2:30 Cleanup and Friday closing circle

3:00 Dismissal

Sample Schedule

Week Two

Middle Grades (3–4)

Week Two

MIDDLE GRADES (3-4)

Community Building and Tone Setting

The message chart

Each morning as children enter the room, they go directly to the chart to read the morning message. It welcomes them and provides an orientation to the day. The ritualized aspect of the morning chart helps establish a sense of predictability and safety for the children. By asking each child to add an idea of her/his own to the chart each morning, children also get the strong message that in this classroom, we value inclusion and participation.

Community Building and Tone Setting

Sharing at Morning Meeting

Building upon the highly structured assigned sharing of summer souvenirs from last week's Morning Meeting, I introduce more open-ended sharing this week, establishing the format we will use all year. Sharing provides an ongoing way for the group to learn more about each other's lives outside of school through structured conversations and dialogue. It teaches important communication skills as the children speak and listen respectfully to one another.

I begin by saying, "Each day in Morning Meeting there will be time for some of us to share news about things in our lives with the class. Everyone will get a chance to share, though not usually every day." We brainstorm appropriate topics for sharing and discuss and model the "jobs" of the sharer—to use a strong voice and to keep the news short and clear. Audience members are expected to listen carefully and respond with respectful, caring questions and comments.

Daily closing circle

I also establish a brief closing ritual at the end of each day during this week. We gather in a circle just before dismissal, and each child has an opportunity to speak a sentence in response to a prompt. Often I prompt, "Tell what you liked best about today" or "Tell one thing you learned today." Depending on the nature of our day together, though, I might sometimes use other prompts, such as "Tell one thing that was hard about today" or "Tell one thing you want to accomplish tomorrow."

Though closing circle lasts only about five minutes, it brings closure and reflection to a hectic time of day. In a low-key way, the circle also recognizes the importance of community by giving us time to say good-bye to each other before going our separate ways. Ending the day in a calm, predictable way is important. We end the day as we began it, our whole group acknowledging and listening to one another.

Choosing outdoor games and debriefing

Outside games continue to be a valuable way to build a sense of the importance of each individual's contribution as well as the power of collaboration. They also provide a needed balance to the demanding cognitive work of the classroom. I generally stick to outdoor games that require only basic skills, such as running and tagging, and ones that are played as a whole group or in teams, so that no individual effort stands out. This makes the games more comfortable and fun for the less athletic children.

A short debriefing at the end of each game facilitates awareness and growth in the social skills involved in playing the game well and enjoying it. At the end of each game, I "circle up" the class and ask for their thoughts on questions such as "What did we do that made this game fun?" or "What was hard about playing this game?" or "What could we do to make it better?" With this daily effort, the children's reflections grow increasingly perceptive, and their sportsmanship and effort visibly improve. I have seen this improvement even in groups that began the year notorious for their competitiveness, bad sportsmanship, and unfriendliness.

Group initiatives

Group initiatives are a kind of game that presents the group as a whole (or smaller subgroups) with a problem to solve. The solution can be reached only with everyone's participation. Group initiatives help children develop skills in cooperation and collaboration, while also providing the sort of intense experience that breaks down barriers between people and builds friendships. Because these initiatives require a certain amount of interdependence and trust to work, I wait until the second (or sometimes third) week of school to begin them.

For this week, I choose short and relatively simple initiatives: "Lean-To," "Everybody Up," "Knots," and "Inchworm." Each exercise takes fifteen minutes or so, leaving plenty of time in the allotted half-hour for debriefing.

If students are really struggling, stopping for a debriefing in the middle of the activity helps enormously.

Simple as these activities are, they can produce a great deal of frustration if a group does not listen to each other and work together. Facilitating them requires patience and a willingness to freeze the action for both encouragement and reflection on the process at key times, so they do not deteriorate into community-damaging experiences rather than community-building ones.

When the initiative is successfully completed, the hard work and perseverance pays off in the sense of pride and accomplishment felt by the group. The group learns an essential truth: when we work hard together, help each other, and persist through difficulty, we succeed. A group that understands this is poised for a tremendous year of learning.

Community Building and Tone Setting

Academic Choice

A kickball challenge

Assuming that the class has shown growth during our outside activities of the week, we will play a game of kickball on Friday. Playing this game successfully with the whole class requires more individual confidence and social skills than were needed for the games played earlier in the week. It is a game often associated with the highly competitive, argumentative, and exclusive playing of traditional recesses. Many children love it and many are intimidated by it. This is a chance to bring the social skills that have been practiced all week into a more challenging arena and to celebrate our growth as a class.

During rehearsing and reflecting times before and after the game, we focus on ways we can take care of each other so everyone can have fun. It is essential for a teacher (me or, when possible, a physical education teacher) to supervise the game closely and stop the action for debriefing if it starts to feel unfriendly. Recess is of enormous importance in children's school lives, and a bad experience during recess has a significant impact upon a child's ability to perform well in school. Therefore, the time spent proactively teaching children to play outside together is invaluable. The skills learned outside will transfer to learning situations inside as well.

Academic Choice

Widening the choices

Children experienced the first steps of working in a choice time last week when they chose among several math games and manipulatives to use during math time. This week, they will work with a wider range of choices in several subject areas. After students have explored ideas about a basic set of materials through guided discoveries, academic choice periods provide more time to explore possibilities and to establish habits for independent work.

Academic choice is also a powerful community builder, allowing a wide range of interests and talents to emerge at the children's initiative. Children who think they have nothing to say to each other discover common interests and become involved in common projects. Often I discover traits and skills in children that I would never have guessed or seen within the boundaries of preset curriculum tasks. We continue to get to know each other better, as students practice working independently in reading, math, writing, and art.

I begin with a sign-up chart listing the possibilities for choice time, all of them familiar from last week's guided discoveries. The number of sign-up slots is important: I make enough slots so that even the last few children to choose have more than one option, yet I make few enough to ensure that children are working in a variety of subject areas.

Goals for choice time

I have two goals for choice times. I want students to experience work in most of the subject areas available during the week, and I want them to keep practicing the rules and procedures for using the materials. While they work at their choices, I observe carefully in order to notice their various skills and interests, and also to coach and keep the children on track with appropriate behavior.

The structure of the choice time and expectations for behavior are clear and continually reinforced. Within that structure, the children engage deeply in the content of their choice. I note the many positives I am sure to see, and I address by reminders and redirections the negatives I will also see. Since the content is open-ended and determined by the children themselves, I am free to put my energy into noticing, reinforcing, and redirecting behavior.

I want students to know what a successful independent working time looks like, feels like, and sounds like. I want them to know how it feels to work with responsibility and engagement, to know without a doubt that they can do it with success. Because I am free to watch them closely, I can keep them on track with encouragement, recognition of their successes, and gentle reminders.

Sharing our work

At the close of each choice time we take about twenty minutes for a work-sharing meeting. Three or four children show their work and tell a bit about it. They then accept a few questions and comments from classmates. Looking at our work together in this way honors and fuels the work. Cognitive growth is enhanced and community is built as students listen and learn and respond to each other.

Often, some of the next day's choice work will build upon the work shared the day before. For example, Rachel's intricate tower built of Cuisenaire® rods might generate a city of towers and vehicles built by a group of children the next day. Jake shares a maze he drew and soon finds himself in the middle of a group of maze drawers—the mazes growing more complex as the students share their ideas. The next day, Alex brings in a book of mazes and the group pores over it together. I often use a few minutes of work-sharing time to reflect on how the choice time went: "What worked well?" or "What was a problem?" and "How could we solve it?"

Academic Choice

Rules and Routines

Through academic choice, students are learning that school is engaging and meaningful to them personally. They learn that they are expected to be active participants, not passive recipients, in learning. They learn that they have many talents and good ideas and that they can be teachers of each other. Not least, they begin to learn that they can follow classroom rules and be responsible, independent workers.

Rules and Routines

Last steps in generating rules

We will finish creating classroom rules this week. Children work in small groups to create proposals for rules that will fit the following criteria:

- They must be general.
- They must be stated in the positive.
- They must be limited to three to five.
- They must cover all the rules we listed in our brainstorm last week.

I find that small groups are the best way to work on this project. I find it hard for all the students to be involved in a whole-group discussion, yet pairs do not allow for enough viewpoints and discussion. Because this is the first time the class has worked in small groups, and because I want them to focus on the content of creating rules more than on the process of working in a small group, I have them use a highly directive worksheet (see sample on the next page).

Thinking About Rules

Group Members:

1. ______________________ **2.** ______________________

3. ______________________ **4.** ______________________

Our class decided that all the rules we thought of fit into four categories. Follow the steps to plan the final draft rules that your group will present to the class.

Category A: Rules about how we treat each other

Step 1: Talk about this category in your group. How could you make one rule that will stand for all the rules we put in this category? (Check the wall chart for the list of rules we thought of.) Stop talking when the bell rings.

Step 2: Group member number one, write your best idea for a rule for this category.

____

Category B: Rules about how we take care of things

Step 1: Talk about this category in your group. How could you make one rule that will stand for all the rules we put in this category? Stop talking when the bell rings.

Step 2: Group member number two, write your best idea for a rule for this category.

____

Category C: Rules about how we do our work

Step 1: Talk about this category in your group. How could you make one rule that will stand for all the rules we put in this category? Stop talking when the bell rings.

Step 2: Group member number three, write your best idea for a rule for this category.

____

Category D: Safety rules

Step 1: Talk about this category in your group. How could you make one rule that will stand for all the rules we put in this category? Stop talking when the bell rings.

Step 2: Group member number four, write your best idea for a rule for this category.

____

Week Two

Middle Grades (3–4)

When we come together as a whole group to compile our small-group lists, we list all the rules by category, and children vote for their favorite rule in each category. Thus, no one group will have developed all our final rules. This helps avoid a sense of competition among groups over whose rules will be adopted.

Applying the rules

Once the rules are decided upon, the focus of much of the week's work is upon applying the rules in a variety of situations. Outside games and initiatives provide lots of opportunities to practice. For example, if one rule says "We will be nice to each other," we discuss and role-play how that might look: "What if someone proposes an idea for getting unknotted in 'Knots' and you're sure it won't work? What will you say or not say that will follow our 'be nice' rule?"

Rules and Routines

Academic choice and the work-sharing component are also sure to provide opportunities to apply and practice the rules. For example, "What can we do if there is only one red marker at a table and two people want to use it for lots of their drawing? If our rule says 'We do our best work,' how would we show that in this situation?"

Introducing quiet time

In addition to practicing routines and procedures introduced last week and applying our new class rules to them, I introduce quiet time and small-group work this week.

Quiet time is a time when students work quietly by themselves. Scheduled right after the active and social times of recess and lunch, it provides some balance in the rhythm of the school day and releases children from the demands of interaction with others. While many children do not think they want or need this release, it serves them well.

This time is intended to be a real release from social interactions, not just a silent time. This means no making faces or communicating by wild gestures to your friend across the room. Seating students far enough apart helps with this. I firmly resist all pleas for exceptions to the work-by-yourself rule. "No, Jenny, you can't practice the spelling words with Alina, even if you whisper really, really quietly—not during quiet time." "No, Charlie, you can't share with Gabe. You have to find your own book for quiet time."

We start simply, with everyone reading a book. Soon I will allow individuals to choose reading, writing, or drawing. Children must gather what they need ahead of time and rely upon their own resources for this time. It is a challenge, and we begin with twenty minutes, working up to half an hour.

As the year progresses, children may use this time to work on assignments or writing projects of their choice. They might enjoy a good book or daydream and doodle. For now, it is enough to practice working alone without talking to others or even asking for help with one's task.

Introducing small-group work

I find that cooperative small-group work challenges children as much as anything I ask them to do in school, yet the amount of learning made possible by small-group work is enormous. I assign children to small groups and change the groupings regularly, providing one more way for children to work with a variety of classmates.

When I first introduce small-group work, I keep the task required of the groups simple, so that they and I can focus on the process. Some small-group work is highly scripted, as with the first rule-making groups. To help the groups ensure that all members are heard, I also give the group protocols such as the "chain reaction" format. This means that one child names his/her idea or question, then turns to the next person, who does the same, and so on around the group circle until everyone has spoken once.

Academics

Launching the formal curricula

While the work we do on rules, procedures, guided discoveries, and community building this week involves many academic skills, it is also important to initiate some of the more formal curricula of the year.

This week I plan to begin spelling instruction (based on the spelling curriculum developed by Rebecca Sitton, *Spelling Sourcebook Series*—see references for a full citation), math instruction (based on the "Investigations in Math" program), and our fall theme study of caves. I choose these three areas because they all involve instruction which is appropriate and engaging for every child in the class, regardless of academic abilities. Each subject area begins with content that calls upon the children's own knowledge and initiative while encouraging them to expand their thinking to the next step.

Spelling

Spelling begins with a review of the thirty most-used words in the English language, words which students will be expected to spell correctly in all their writing after this week. Most of the words are already familiar, and even the poorest spellers can read the words on the board and locate them in their own writing. More adept students who write fluently will have more words to locate, while less adept writers will naturally have fewer.

Academics

Beginning the math curriculum

Commonly referred to as "Investigations" or "Investigations in Math," this curriculum is formally titled *Investigations in Number, Data, and Space* and was developed in 1998 by the Technical Education Research Center (TERC) in Cambridge, Massachusetts with the support of the National Science Foundation (see references for a full citation).

The first lessons in the "Investigations" math curriculum ask students to use multilink cubes (which they have already worked with in guided discovery and choice) to build objects and then estimate how many cubes they used. All students can estimate, though some are much more sophisticated in their strategies than others. There is opportunity to set up small groups here, so that more and less sophisticated mathematicians can work together. Over the course of the week, everyone grows in estimating skills and math concepts.

Beginning our cave study

I find caves a great theme for beginning the year. There is much geography and science connected with them; they are also mysterious, even a bit scary. Learning information that explains some of the mysteries and dispels some of the fear (perhaps even going on a safely challenging "caving" expedition) appeals to this age group's adventurous and inquisitive spirit. It establishes that they will be doing grown-up and rigorous work, tackling topics that are truly demanding.

We begin our study in the pair-share format by brainstorming facts that we know about caves. Partners report back to the larger group, and together we compile a pretty impressive list. Next, using the "chain reaction" format in small groups, we generate questions we have about caves. After this, I will read aloud *Caves and Caverns* by Gail Gibbons (San Diego: Harcourt Brace & Company, 1993) and small groups will list and report to the whole group what they learned from the book.

Small-group work is central to this process, and I take care to make sure that all assignments are accessible at various levels. All children can share ideas, think of a question, and remember something from a read-aloud book, though they are operating from a wide range of skill and knowledge bases. I am vigilant throughout these theme times to make sure that students show cooperation and respect for each other's contributions as well as focusing upon the tasks involved.

Theme choice projects

The assignment at the end of the week—to use the materials in the room to represent something they learned about caves this week—integrates the learning from guided discoveries and activity time as well as the content from our theme study. First, I ask students to brainstorm a list of ways they could show what they have learned using media available in the room at this point: blocks, crayons, markers, colored pencils, cubes, and Cuisenaire® rods. After contemplating this list of possibilities, students choose what method they will use and check in with me about it. Then they make a plan using a worksheet such as the one shown below. This planning process requires students to articulate what they will be doing and to anticipate materials and resources they will need as well as where they will work. Upon completing their projects, they will present their work to the rest of the class.

Week Two

Middle Grades (3–4)

Academic Choice Project

Name: ______________________ **Date:** __________

MY PLAN

Our Content Area is: ______________________

I will: ______________________

____

A skill I'll be working on is: ______________________

Materials I'll need are: ______________________

____

Where I'll work is: ______________________

If I need to find out more, I'll: ______________________

____

I have partner(s): ☐ **No** ☐ **Yes**

I'll work with: ______________________

Day Six

8:30 Arrival and morning message: message asks children to write ideas about "What makes lunch fun for everyone?"

8:45 Morning Meeting

Greeting: "Roll Call"
Introduce sharing
Activity: "Electricity"
Morning Message

9:15 Social studies

Introduce and model timelines

Brainstorm possible events students might include in personal timelines

Students begin making personal timelines

10:00 Outside: trust initiative—"Inchworm"

10:30 Rule-making: small groups brainstorm a list of rules that will help them accomplish their hopes and dreams, and then share their lists with the whole group

11:30 Outside: play "Silly Soccer"

12:00 Lunch

12:30 Lunch sharing and check-in

12:40 Read-aloud

1:00 Language arts: begin independent reading projects

2:30 Cleanup and journal writing

2:50 Closing circle

3:00 Dismissal

Day Seven

8:30 Arrival and morning message: message contains riddles about classmates that children can write answers to as they read the chart

9:15 Morning Meeting

Greeting: introduce the option of choosing which classmate to greet
Sharing
Activity: "Category Snap"
Morning Message

9:45 Social studies

Complete personal timelines

Homework: "What countries did your ancestors come from? Interview a parent or adult relative to find out. Be prepared to share with the class."

10:00 Outside: trust initiative—"Mirror Image"

10:20 Rule-making

Whole-group lesson on creating categories for the lists of rules from yesterday

Small groups create three to five categories for their rules

10:50 Math games

11:30 Outside: play "Kick and Catch"

12:00 Lunch

12:30 Lunch check-in

1:00 Language arts

Independent reading projects

Introduce spelling books and first lesson

2:30 Cleanup and journal writing

2:50 Closing circle

3:00 Dismissal

Day Eight

8:30 Arrival and morning message: message will ask students to write the names of the countries their ancestors came from

8:45 Morning Meeting

Greeting: same as yesterday (choose a classmate to greet)
Sharing
Activity: "Hot Potato"
Morning Message

9:15 Social studies: sharing personal timelines in small groups and whole group

10:00 Outside: trust initiative—"Human Camera"

10:20 Rule-making: small groups create proposal for three to five classroom rules to present to class

10:50 Math games

11:30 Outside: play "Continuous Kickball"

12:00 Lunch

12:30 Lunch check-in and read-aloud

1:00 Language arts: continue independent reading projects and daily spelling

2:30 Cleanup and journal writing

2:50 Closing circle

3:00 Dismissal

Sample Schedule

Week Two

Upper Grades (5–6)

Day Nine

8:30 Arrival and morning chart: chart has jumbled spelling words for children to unscramble

8:45 Morning Meeting

Greeting: choose a classmate to greet
Sharing
Activity: "Twenty Questions"
Morning Message

9:15 Social studies: interview planning

Homework: Interview a parent or adult relative about a memory they have from when they were 11 or 12 years old.

10:00 Outside: trust initiative—"Everybody Up"

10:20 Rule-making: small groups present proposal for three to five rules, and class votes on final set of rules

11:00 Math assessment

11:30 Outside: play "Bombardment"

12:00 Lunch

12:30 Lunch check-in and read-aloud

1:00 Language arts

2:30 Cleanup and journal writing

3:00 Dismissal

Day Ten

8:30 Arrival and morning chart: message asks children to write one interesting fact they learned in their homework interviews

8:45 Morning Meeting

Greeting: choose a classmate to greet
Sharing
Activity: "Grandmother's Trunk"
Morning Message

9:15 Social studies

Introduce standards and procedures for "final draft" work

Students write homework interviews in final draft form

10:00 Outside: group initiative—"Platform"

10:30 Math: graphing activity

11:30 Outside: play "Capture the Flag"

12:00 Lunch

12:30 Lunch check-in and read-aloud

1:00 Language arts

2:30 Appreciation circle

3:00 Dismissal

Week Two

UPPER GRADES (5-6)

Community Building and Tone Setting

Morning Meeting greeting

Community Building and Tone Setting

We begin this week with a new greeting—"Roll Call." It consists of a rhythmic chant in which each participant declares his/her name and nickname and a personal talent or positive identity (such as student, friend, athlete, singer), to which the entire group responds in chorus. Each person receives attention and acknowledgment from the entire class, and it's a great refresher course in students' names. It's also an upbeat way to start the week and fifth- and sixth-graders especially enjoy the rap-like beat.

Beginning on Tuesday, I hand over another responsibility to the group—that of choosing whom they will greet at Morning Meeting. The actual greeting will remain a simple "Good Morning, ________," so that we can focus our attention on the issues that arise around choosing which classmate to greet.

I ask the class, "If our greetings are to make everyone in our class feel welcome, what are some things you will need to keep in mind as you choose whom to greet?" Children this age know exactly what is hard about making such decisions!

"It helps not to just pick your best friends," says one.

"No one should laugh or tease if a boy greets a girl or a girl greets a boy. It doesn't mean you have a crush," says another.

"It won't feel good if the same people are always greeted last. Try to mix up the order people are greeted."

"We could try to greet someone we haven't talked to lately," suggests yet another.

We give it a try. Despite the wisdom and genuine good intentions shown in our pre-greeting discussion, the actual greeting usually demonstrates a few of the very actions they've just said they wanted to avoid. After our first try, I ask them to reflect upon what they did well and what they could do better.

Greeting each other daily in a friendly, inclusive way can be more of a challenge to older elementary students than to younger students, and patience is often required. However, insisting on a high standard of interaction during this simple daily event is critical to the development of a powerful sense of community. If I sense that greetings are slipping past relaxed and into sloppy or perfunctory behaviors, I remind the group of the standards set in our initial discussion and of the reasons why warm and respectful greetings are important. Students are developing key habits and attitudes that carry over into other aspects of the school day.

Introducing sharing

Week Two

Upper Grades (5-6)

I introduce sharing by telling about something I did the previous weekend. "After you listen," I tell the students, "I want you to see how many questions and comments you can think of which show respectful interest."

"On Saturday, I went to the Museum of Fine Arts and saw an exhibit of paintings by an artist named Martin Johnson Heade. I'm ready for your questions and comments."

Lively questions abound. How did I get to the museum? What kind of artist was this Heade? Modern? Old-fashioned? Did he use oil paint? Watercolor? Where and when did he live? Had I ever heard of him before I went?

One comment is offered: "It sounds like you like to go to art shows." Offering comments is often harder than asking questions, and we will work on it during the year. We are off to a good start.

Afterward, I ask students to comment on what I did to make sharing interesting and easy for them to respond to. We talk about the purposes of sharing (to get to know and enjoy each other more), and we brainstorm possible topics for sharing. Ideas usually include family stories, hobbies, current events, extracurricular activities, etc. I list and post these topic ideas for easy reference.

On subsequent days, students will have an opportunity to share. For this week, I'll arrange student sharing by asking for two or three volunteers who will plan to share the following day. I check in with those students in the morning before our meeting to ascertain the appropriateness of their topic before they share. I might help reshape sharing that is really "bragging," check with parents before certain family news is announced to the class, or veto "humorous" sharing about a hurtful prank.

Making lunch fun

The question on the morning message chart on Monday—"What makes lunch fun for everyone?"—launches a discussion designed to give students more responsibility for a positive lunch experience. Until now, I have maintained a great deal of control over what students do at lunch. Now, with careful planning, the children will begin to take conscious control of what happens socially during lunch. Near the end of the first Morning Meeting this week, we read and talk about the ideas students have written on the chart about what makes lunch fun for everyone, adding any new ideas that come up.

The operative phrase here is "fun for everyone." If I, or any student, doubt whether a particular lunch goal or behavior is fun *for everyone,* I ask students to rethink and rephrase the idea until we all agree that it will work. I find that with children of this age, it is often necessary and effective at this stage for me to offer my perspective and experience and to make rulings.

For example, "We could sit wherever we want" is a common suggestion. If I were to ask whether this would be fun for them all, it would be very difficult, especially this early in the year, for those less popular to speak up and describe the discomfort of being "the leftovers." Instead, I respond to the idea by saying, "I know, for me, if I am at the end of a cafeteria line and I see a lot of people in my group heading toward a table, it makes me feel worried that I won't have people to eat with. So I'm going to strike that one."

For the rest of the week, this morning's chart, full of ideas for ways to have a fun lunchtime, will hang on the wall. After each lunch, we will gather for a debriefing on how successful lunch was for everyone, noting which of the ideas were used from the chart. I do not expect that every lunchtime will be wonderful for everybody, but I do expect students to reflect upon what worked and what didn't, and to get better and better at taking good care of themselves and each other during lunch.

If lunch is particularly problematic, we might extend our discussion into read-aloud time in order to develop strategies for improving the next lunchtime. These kinds of reflections and follow-up plans are critical. Holding initial discussions and naming expectations are just the first step in letting my students know that I really believe in their ability to be inclusive. I not only believe in their ability, but I will hold them to high standards of achievement, and I will help them get there.

Group initiatives

Group initiatives, also important in developing the classroom community, occur daily this week. For the first four days, the focus is upon trust-building activities in pairs. The initiative "Inchworm" requires pairs to move across space while their feet and hands are attached. "Mirror Image" asks pairs to stand face-to-face while one partner observes closely to imitate the other's movements simultaneously, as though looking in a mirror. Both partners need to tune in closely to each other to succeed at this.

In "Human Camera," one partner is led blindfolded by the other to a spot. The leading partner "focuses" the blindfolded one on a particular scene of choice, such as a flower or landscape, then briefly removes the blindfold so the partner can view the "picture." The blindfold is then replaced. Each partner may take several "pictures." At the end of each round, partners discuss the experience and share impressions of the "pictures" taken. "Everybody Up" requires skills similar to those used in "Inchworm," but it may be made more difficult with the addition of threesomes and foursomes. These trust initiatives are simple and short and are always followed by a five- to ten-minute debriefing period in which strategies and feelings about the process are discussed.

These partner activities lay the groundwork necessary for the group to tackle more challenging problem-solving group initiatives, ones that require not just two or three but the entire group to listen to each other and work together. On Day Ten, I introduce the first such initiative, which will probably require at least thirty minutes. The challenge is to try to get everyone in the class onto a three-foot by three-foot platform or space. This takes a great deal of patience, creativity, and cooperation. If the group cannot complete the task in twenty minutes, we will stop the action, debrief on what is working and what isn't, and try again another day. If they do complete the task in twenty minutes, we debrief about the process just the same. Another time, they can try to squeeze everyone on an even smaller platform!

Appreciation circle

The appreciation circle introduced on Day Ten will become the regular closing circle on the last day of each week. Appreciation circles provide structured weekly practice in noticing and valuing each other's strengths and in giving and receiving compliments.

During Morning Meeting on Friday, each student draws another's name from a hat, without revealing it to classmates. I tell students to think about and secretly observe the person whose name they drew throughout the day, and to be prepared to offer that person a sincere appreciation (something that she/he did which you appreciate) or compliment during the closing circle. I emphasize that the appreciation needs to be for something the person did, rather than for something such as his/her appearance or a possession.

While in the circle, each person takes a turn to shake the hand of the student he/she has been observing and to deliver the appreciation. The receiving student may say nothing or may say "thank you." Appreciation circles end our week together on a positive note!

Rules and Routines

Community Building and Tone Setting

Rules and Routines

Creating the rules

The process of creating, categorizing, and agreeing upon rules capitalizes on the fifth- and sixth-grader's love of debate, justice, and student rights. We spend time throughout the week creating rules (see sample schedule for this week). While many of the sessions begin with a meeting of the entire group, most of the discussion and development of rules occurs in small groups where everyone can be maximally involved. I expect lots of fervent opinions to be voiced as the young people decide upon categories for rules they've brainstormed, and then again as they work to articulate and agree upon the wording of their final three to five rules.

Structures to help group discussion

An important part of this work is the discussion of structures that will help group members listen and speak to each other respectfully and find ways to reach consensus. Before each small-group session, we discuss the format we will use, such as each group member taking a role (note-taker, timekeeper, active listener, facilitator, etc.) or simply taking turns around the circle. These small-group sessions provide students with intensive practice working in cooperative groups while allowing them to brainstorm, listen to, and discuss many perspectives about what rules are for and how they are best worded.

A vote on the rules

When the class is finally ready on Day Ten to vote on a final set of rules, they do so from a base of much thought and active debate. Before the final vote, I post all the rules from every group. Then, students privately vote for the three they think will make the best complete set. Depending on how the vote goes, I announce the three, four, or five rules receiving the most votes as our final set. Student volunteers make posters of these rules—a set for our room and a set to take to specials in other rooms.

Academics

All of the curriculum this week, including the rule-making, consists of fairly open-ended activities which allow me to focus upon getting to know my students while they continue to get to know each other. Instruction is short and to the point. Students are able to work independently alone and in small groups, and I am able to oversee the whole group, coaching and reinforcing behavior.

Independent reading projects

The reading curriculum for the next four or five weeks will consist of "independent reading projects." Our guided discovery of the classroom library last week, including selection of a book to read, laid the groundwork for this. During silent reading time last week, I checked in with each student either to confirm his/her final choice or to ask him/her to choose another book upon which we could agree.

Students read their book for at least thirty minutes each night for homework and for fifteen minutes during language arts time. During the rest of language arts time, students work on tasks outlined in reading project packets. These project packets, which I revise each year, consist of activities such as adding vocabulary words to a student-created glossary or writing character sketches for the main characters with descriptions, quotes, and drawings. Other assignments involve plot, setting, theme, and the application of ideas in the book to the student's own experience. A culminating activity requires students to work with these components as they develop their own original short stories.

This approach to reading and writing instruction works especially well during the first six weeks of school as students learn about class routines and expectations and I learn about students and their reading and writing skills. As in other curricula chosen or designed for these weeks, the assignments allow students to work independently at their own level. After my brief check-in or mini-lesson each day, the project packet directs the children's activities, so I am free to keep an overview. I watch, listen, coach behavior, and check in with individuals, building relationships. This is not a time of intensive instruction on my part. The project activities, mini-lessons, and the book being read instruct, while I gather information about students and coach.

Spelling lessons

Spelling lessons also begin this week, guided by a workbook. Once I introduce the workbook, students work on daily lessons with independence. I begin each week with a mini-lesson on the week's words and include one or two more mini-lessons during the week. Workbook pages can be completed in school or for homework.

Academics

Math games and assessment

Math continues with math games providing excellent practice and review of computation and problem-solving skills, while allowing learners with a wide range of skills to work and play together. As in language arts, I am able to use most of math time to interact with individuals and observe students' skills and styles of dealing with mathematical tasks. As the week progresses and the children relax a bit, I give a more formal math assessment that allows me to begin planning to work with students in small groups in the future.

A graphing activity

By Day Ten, I am ready to begin more formal instruction with the introduction of a graphing activity. We start by looking at some graphs from magazines and newspapers, and small groups list all the things they notice about them. The groups discuss questions such as "What do all these graphs have in common?" or "What types of information do they give?" or "How do you think they were created?" Together we think about what kind of information can be graphed and what kind can't.

Over the next days and weeks, students identify information they'd like to learn about classmates and try their hand at data collection and making their own graphs. As they gain experience using different graphing styles, they also begin to collect information from students beyond their own classroom. They learn about random sampling and report their findings on the school population as a whole.

I know a unit on graphing will provide an appropriate challenge to all the students in my class, because each one can choose to collect information of personal interest and can choose from a variety of ways to graph that information—

from simple bar graphs to more complex line graphs that plot trends or compare two related sets of information. While they learn math, they also learn more about each other. As students create their graphs, I circulate and oversee, just as in language arts.

Social studies

In social studies, the approach is similar, only here the organizational tool is the timeline, as students focus upon their own histories and those of their families. Even in fifth and sixth grade, a study of the long ago and far away is best begun with the student's own experience. I introduce social studies by asking students to look at their own lives as history. Students look for the ties their families might have to other parts of the world and interview relatives as resources on history and geography. The work of the first couple of weeks of social studies introduces basic concepts about the study of history, teaching some techniques historians use, such as interviewing, documentation, and the study of artifacts. These concepts and techniques will support the study of explorers and exploration we will undertake later in the fall. Additionally, while history comes alive for the students, they continue to learn more about themselves and each other.

Week Three

CHAPTER THREE

I *often think of the picture book* Make Way for Ducklings *during these early weeks. I feel like the mama duck tending her charges as they make their uneven way across the street. In the first two weeks, I have led them through each day with a careful eye and tremendous care, redirecting and encouraging frequently. By now they can all safely "cross the street" and are ready to make short flights on their own. But as with all beginners, they will sometimes fall. I provide the safety net, loose enough to let them experiment, tight enough to keep them from harm.*

PAULA DENTON, *teacher*

While the image of teachers as hovering mother ducks is not our overall professional ideal, there is something about it that fits the earliest weeks of the year. In fact, it is this very close attention and direction that will allow enormous independence and impressive flights later in the year.

During the first two weeks of school, we maintained a high degree of external control in the classroom by planning structures that allowed us to watch and coach the entire group at all times. We provided learning experiences along with reflection and analysis of these experiences, raising children's awareness of how they can be positive and productive members of the classroom community.

This week we are settling into a more predictable schedule. We have repeatedly taught and modeled all the basic routines and expectations, and the children have practiced them many times. The emphasis on reflection and discussion continues as the children grow in their ability to think about their own behavior and how it affects others. Now, in the third week, we provide more and more room for students to make choices and try out their independence, encouraging internalization of the rules and expectations that were so clearly defined and articulated in the first two weeks.

Activity time in the primary grades, for example, evolves into academic choice time, with students deciding which of many activities to choose. At Morning Meeting, varied greetings and cooperative activities such as "Zoom" and "Coseeki," which require more initiative and responsibility, are introduced. If outdoor play is generally friendly and peaceful, we might offer free play or "choice" on the playground at some of the recesses. We also give children more input about where they will sit during meetings and work times.

Overview

We want to move the group toward increased responsibility and independence in following the rules and routines of the class without continual, direct teacher supervision. This independence allows teachers to concentrate on instruction and observation in order to provide the best learning opportunities for each child in the class. As a group, we discuss the purposes of independent work times and explore the different choices and decisions that children can make during these times. We begin by asking, "Why do we have choice time in school?" or "Why is your choice time work important in our class?"

To give children practice in working independently, while the teacher is still providing a "safety net," we use a teaching strategy that we call "the paradox." The teacher works with a small group of children, while the rest of the group is working on independent work. However, the teacher makes sure that the small-group work requires very little of the teacher's attention (although it shouldn't be just busywork). While appearing to be focused upon the small group, the teacher really is keeping a close eye on the whole class (this is the paradox), monitoring students' progress in working independently and guiding them when necessary.

There is much preparation that precedes these independent work periods, including discussions which emphasize students' responsibilities. Students must understand the expectations for independent work. They will

- plan ahead what they will do,
- use quiet voices,
- stay focused on their work, and
- try to solve problems they encounter by themselves or with the help of their peers.

Then we remind, reinforce, and redirect as needed. As the work period begins, the teacher might ask, "What will you need to think about so that you can work for this whole period?"

"Yes, you need to choose a good place to sit for the work you are going to do."

"Yes, bring everything you will need."

"Yes, get a drink before you get settled."

"And if you finish early, what can you do?"

Students' ability to manage themselves and help each other when they are not working directly with a teacher is essential to the success of independent work periods and to the overall well-being of the classroom.

Another central goal this week is to make the rules (which the class worked to create) come alive in daily practice. An important part of establishing a tone of participation, responsibility, and trust in the classroom is sending a very clear message about the rules: "The rules, which we have all worked so hard to create and agree upon, provide the daily living backbone of our classroom culture. They are real. They are important. They can be counted upon to guide us to high standards both in learning and in behaving ethically."

This week, we devote ourselves to establishing this truth in the minds of the students as irrevocably as possible. We refer to the rules frequently in the context of daily activities and lessons, asking children to think of behaviors in particular situations that would exhibit "following the rules." The concrete application of abstract rules to specific situations is crucial.

Some of our group reflections about how various activities are going will generate topics for role-playing (see Key Terms for a description of this teaching strategy). The strategy of role-playing is similar to modeling, though it is a bit more elaborate and calls for greater input from the children. Role-plays expand children's perspectives on situations and facilitate internalization of rules.

In role-plays, we ask children to imagine and share ways they might interpret the rules in a specific problem situation. This requires them to practice thinking for themselves and to actively apply the rules to many parts of their experience at school, from "butts" in the lunch line to finding help when they're stuck on a math problem. We rarely need to schedule role-plays in our weekly planning because their content and timing arise organically out of daily events.

For example, if we observe a wide range of handwriting abilities in class, knowing that nine-year-olds can be very competitive, we might role-play ways to encourage a classmate who is less skilled in this area. This might come during

Morning Meeting on the day of a handwriting lesson, or as part of introducing new handwriting workbooks.

Much of our energy in these early weeks is focused on establishing expectations and boundaries, creating a climate of acceptance and respect, and helping children ponder and rehearse positive ways to behave. But we also know that mistakes will be made—must be made, in fact, if children are to extend their knowledge and learning. Assignments will be sloppily done, students will come to math group without materials, children will be turned away from games even though there's plenty of room for another player.

Our approach to discipline must be reactive as well as proactive. We want our reactions to these mistakes to help children identify and learn from them. This week, we introduce logical consequences, a cornerstone of our reactive approach to discipline.

Overview

By the end of the third week, the daily schedule is familiar and predictable and is close to what will be an ongoing regular schedule. The classroom climate is becoming comfortable, nurturing, and orderly. We have introduced all the components of Morning Meeting. And we have held important conversations revolving around the rules generated and agreed upon last week, exploring their application and establishing a basic understanding of what will happen when rules are broken. Expectations for small-group and independent work have been established, and children are working to meet them.

Even when things are going smoothly, teachers must still pay close attention. They must notice and encourage the many wonderful, specific ways students care for themselves and others and give them feedback when they are not showing that good care and helpfulness. The efforts required of students to meet the expectations of a new school year are great; our best attention and recognition is required to support them.

Goals for Week Three

The goals for the third week of school are the following:

- **With less direct teacher supervision than in Weeks One and Two, most children will be participating successfully in the regular routines of the room, and in whole-group, small-group, and independent work formats.**

- **Children will think critically about ways to follow the class rules. Role-playing in addition to discussion, modeling, and practice will help children apply the rules to a variety of specific troublesome situations arising in the course of the day.**

- **Students will be able to work independently while the teacher is working with a small group (using "the paradox" strategy).**

- **Logical consequences will be introduced, discussed, and rehearsed.**

- **Children will participate in curriculum in each major subject area. Curricular activities will be stopped for reflection and redirection as often as needed for the group to succeed at both social and academic expectations.**

- **Specialist teachers continue to join the class and work together with classroom teachers to create joint, integrated expectations and to share knowledge about the children.**

Goals for Week Three

Day Eleven

8:30 **Arrival and morning chart**

8:45 **Morning Meeting:** introduce logical consequences with song "I'm Gonna Tell"

9:15 **Math:** multilink cube activities

10:00 **Outside game**

10:30 **Snack**

10:45 **Introduce time-out**

11:30 **Outside**

12:00 **Lunch**

12:30 **Story time**

12:50 **Quiet time**

1:15 **Language arts:** self-portrait

2:00 **Academic choice:** introduction

2:45 **Closing circle**

3:00 **Dismissal**

Day Twelve

8:30 **Arrival and morning chart**

8:45 **Morning Meeting:** introduce activity—"Zoom"

9:15 **Math**

10:00 **Outside game**

10:30 **Snack**

10:45 **Science:** "Spider Hunt" outside

11:30 **Outside**

12:00 **Lunch**

12:30 **Story time**

12:50 **Quiet time:** begin individual reading assessments

1:15 **Language arts:** self-portraits

2:00 **Academic choice:** role-play working independently while teacher is busy

2:45 **Closing circle**

3:00 **Dismissal**

Day Thirteen

8:30 **Arrival and morning chart**

8:45 **Morning Meeting**
Teach new greeting: "Buenos Días"
Activity: "Hot and Cold"

9:15 **Math**

10:00 **Outside game**

10:30 **Snack**

10:45 **Science:** observations of spiders found yesterday

11:30 **Outside**

12:00 **Lunch**

12:30 **Story time**

12:50 **Quiet time:** assessments

1:15 **Language arts:** self-portraits

2:00 **Academic choice:** book bags with small group

2:45 **Closing circle**

3:00 **Dismissal**

Sample Schedule

Week Three

Primary Grades (K–2)

Day Fourteen

8:30 **Arrival and morning chart**

8:45 **Morning Meeting:** activity—play "Follow the Sound"

9:15 **Math**

10:00 **Outside game**

10:30 **Snack**

10:45 **Science:** "Spider Hunt" outside

11:30 **Outside**

12:00 **Lunch**

12:30 **Story time**

12:50 **Quiet time**

1:15 **Language arts:** self-portraits

2:00 **Academic choice:** book bags with small group

2:45 **Closing circle**

3:00 **Dismissal**

Day Fifteen

8:30 **Arrival and morning chart**

8:45 **Morning Meeting**
New greeting: "Hello" with handshake
Activity: "Coseeki"

9:15 **Math**

10:00 **Outside game**

10:30 **Snack**

10:45 **Science:** spider observations

11:30 **Outside**

12:00 **Lunch**

12:30 **Story time**

12:50 **Quiet time**

1:15 **Language arts:** self-portraits

2:00 **Academic choice:** book bags with small group

2:45 **Closing circle**

3:00 **Dismissal**

Week Three

PRIMARY GRADES (K–2)

Community Building and Tone Setting

Varying greetings

If the children are using clear, friendly voices and making eye contact with the simple "Good Morning" greeting, they are ready for some variations. The first variation, on Day Thirteen, varies only in the language used to say "Good Morning." I chose Spanish, since it is a language some of my students know, but any language that reflects the families and interests of the group is fine.

Community Building and Tone Setting

As the year progresses, we will learn greetings in several languages, and the children will have opportunities to choose which greeting they would like to use on a given day. For now, we just add Spanish. Along with "Good Morning," I write "Buenos Días" on a wall chart within view of the meeting area.

By Friday, we might be ready for a bit more variety in our greeting. "Hello" is a song we might sing for the greeting:

"Hello! Hello! Hello, and how are you?"

"I'm fine! I'm fine, and I hope that you are too!"

The children divide into an inner and an outer circle so that each child faces a partner. As we sing the song, we shake hands with our partner. Then the people in the inner circle move to the left and shake hands with a new person, singing the song once again. We continue in this way until each child in the inner circle has shaken hands and sung with each child in the outer circle. This greeting allows children repeated opportunities to practice friendly greetings with many classmates in a playful way. Once learned, it joins the list of greetings on our wall chart.

Morning Meeting activities

Up until now, cooperative activities at Morning Meeting have consisted of learning and singing songs together. We will continue singing all year from time to time, but now we are ready to learn other kinds of cooperative activities and games that require more personal initiative and responsibility from the children.

"Zoom" is a perfect beginning game, as it blends the choral unison of singing with the individual initiative needed in a game. Participants simply pass the word "zoom" around the circle one at a time. The person who begins the game turns to a neighbor and says, "zoom." The receiver of the "zoom" then turns and passes it on to the next person. The first challenge is for everyone to pass the "zoom" flawlessly and smoothly around the circle. It might take a few tries! Once that is mastered, children enjoy timing themselves to see how quickly they can pass the "zoom" completely around once, then twice.

The game of "Hot and Cold" is also quite simple and a good choice for early this week. While a volunteer leaves the sight of the group, a child in the circle chooses a place to hide an object. When the volunteer returns, she/he begins to search the room for the object while the class gives feedback. If the seeker is close to the object, the class shouts "hot!" and if far away, the class shouts "cold!" Gradations such as warm, lukewarm, and cool may be used as well. This continues until the seeker finds the object. I try to have time for two or three seekers to find an object during one play session.

"Follow the Sound," which I plan to introduce on Day Fourteen, is similar to "Zoom" in that a sound is passed around the circle, but in this game the children have more choices to make. Each child mimics the sound passed from the previous child, then creates a new sound to pass to the next child in the circle.

"Coseeki," which I hope to teach on Day Fifteen, is the most challenging game introduced this week. In this game, the children must closely watch and follow the motions of a selected classmate "leader" while trying not to divulge who that leader is. A volunteer, who was absent during selection of the leader, stands in the middle of the circle and tries to guess who is leading the group.

Students choose seating

In addition to varying greetings and adding cooperative games to Morning Meeting activities, the teacher can give increased responsibility to groups that are ready for it by allowing children input into where they will sit during meetings and work times.

As a first step, I might have students draw numbers, colors, or shapes from a basket that match labels on seats, or I might ask them to sit together by category (eye color, sock color, birthday months, etc.). A next step, requiring more personal responsibility, is to ask children to sit according to more open-ended criteria, such as "Sit boy, girl" or "Sit next to someone you haven't worked or played with lately." Although each class varies in its readiness to assume this responsibility, I hope to reach this point at some time during this week.

Choice at recess time

Outside time continues to be important for community building. This week, we continue to play cooperative games during the mid-morning outside time. I also have children play cooperative games during the regularly scheduled recess time at 11:30 if they still seem to need a high degree of structure and supervision to enjoy a friendly, peaceful recess time. If they seem ready to handle more freedom, they have free play or a choice of several games on the playground. Recess provides wonderful opportunities for the group to try their wings at following the class rules on their own. It is important, however, that a teacher watch closely and be prepared to redirect children or use consequences as necessary, so that the tone of recess time remains primarily positive and friendly for all students.

Rules and Logical Consequences

Rules and Logical Consequences

Introducing logical consequences

I plan to spend about ten minutes introducing logical consequences during the activity time of Morning Meeting on Day Eleven. We begin by singing the song "I'm Gonna Tell on You" by Rosalie Sorrels (see Appendix E for song reference).

"I'm gonna tell, oh I'm gonna tell.
I'm gonna holler and I'm gonna yell.
I'll get you in trouble for everything you do.
I'm gonna tell on you!"

From this chorus, the verses of the song move on to list lots of awful things a child might do that could "get you in trouble," such as eating all the cookies and "busting" a plate. I find that beginning with this song brings a tone of warmth and humor to the topic and helps children begin to think about rule-breaking behavior with compassion and a constructive attitude.

After we enjoy the song together, I ask the children how many of them have ever seen someone "mess up" or break a rule. A few of them share their experiences. Then I ask, "Has anyone in this class ever broken a rule or done something they shouldn't?" I raise my hand in response to that question, and, given the tone of the discussion, most, if not all, of the children raise hands too.

"Of course!" I say. "Everyone makes mistakes sometimes. That's one way we learn—by making mistakes and then fixing them. When you make a mistake in our class, I'll help you fix it. I'll talk with you about what you need to do to fix that mistake so you can learn. If you are having a hard time following the rules, I might tell you to stop doing something for awhile so you can get back in control of yourself."

If there is time, we generate a few examples of what it might look and sound like to make a mistake and fix it. If there is not enough time now, I will use time later in the day. This introduction aims primarily to set an open, nonjudgmental tone concerning consequences for misbehavior, while reinforcing high expectations and clear limits for behavior.

Teaching time-out

Later that same morning, I'll focus on teaching the procedure I use for time-out. I use time-out as a logical consequence when a child is disrupting a group or needs to regain self-control in order to follow the rules of the room. When introducing time-out to the children, I emphasize the important idea that time-out is not intended to be a time to feel bad about yourself. It is a time to take a few breaths, relax, calm down, and get ready to go back, with better self-control, to the activity which you left. This year, I will call time-out "rest stop."

As a group, we might share ideas about what kinds of thoughts help us calm down. Children might mention looking out the window or daydreaming, practicing counting, or planning what they will have for a snack when they get home.

We then begin practicing the rest stop procedure, with a child volunteering to demonstrate what it will look like to go to the rest stop. I say "rest stop" to that child and he/she walks calmly to sit in the designated place. He/she chooses one of the strategies we've listed for directing his/her thoughts while sitting for a minute. When cued by me to return to the group, the child walks calmly back and rejoins the ongoing activity. I ask, "What did you notice that was helpful about the way Joanna went to our rest stop?" The children name the helpful behaviors displayed:

"She didn't talk to anybody, just walked and sat."

"She looked out the window."

"When you said 'rest stop,' she just got up and went there."

"What were her hands and feet doing in the rest stop?" I might ask.

"Just being still."

The volunteer then shares what he/she thought about while sitting. During the rest of the meeting time, some of the children will have a turn to practice going to the rest stop in a helpful way. We make a game of it and applaud each child's performance.

When the teacher makes a mistake

Before the practice session ends, I tell children about a couple of important issues that will likely surface in the use of rest stop. I might say, "Teachers can make mistakes too. Sometimes I might tell you to go to the rest stop when you are really following the rules and you don't really need a rest stop. If I do that to you, I need you to just go anyway, but after you come back, and our lesson is done, you can let me know you want to tell me about that. Or, if you don't know why I told you to go to the rest stop, you can ask me why after the lesson is over."

If the students know that they will have an opportunity to question me or inform me of a sense of injustice, they are more likely to go to time-out gracefully when told. If I do find that I have made a mistake, I make an apology.

Rules and Logical Consequences

Academics

Academics

Academic choice

Activity time evolves into academic choice time this week. The children are used to the process of putting a check on the chart beside the activity I assign them during activity time. Now it is a simple step to announcing which activity they have chosen and then placing a check beside it on the chart before going off to work. Behind this simple step, however, is a more complex skill—that of making a good choice.

I ask for the children's ideas about why we have activity time and choice time in school. Together we list the reasons:

"To get to try new things."

"To get good ideas from each other."

"To spend time working on something you really care about."

"To get better at something you really want to learn like drawing or math."

As part of the introduction of choice time, I lead the children in a discussion of what to consider when deciding which activity to pursue. "If we are going to be able to choose activities that will help us learn and get to know each other and find out new things about ourselves, what will we need to think about when we make a choice?" I ask. Their responses are usually quite thoughtful.

"Don't just pick something because your friend is doing it."

"Sometimes it is good to try something you think you don't like to do, because you might find out you like it."

"You shouldn't do the same thing every single day."

I tell the children that sometimes some of them will have "have-tos" during choice time. That will happen when I want to work with a small group on a special project or lesson, or when I decide that some children need to spend time on an activity they haven't chosen to do on their own. Mainly, though, the choice will be truly theirs.

As with activity time, choices are limited to activities that have been introduced in guided discoveries. I try to provide four to eight activities from which to choose at any one choice time. Once choice time is well established, I occasionally use this time to bring guided discoveries of new, more specialized activities, such as easel painting, block building, and drama corner, to small groups while others engage in their choices. These new activities then become part of choice time, while other activities may be removed.

Building autonomy: a role-play on independent work

A focus this week is upon helping children develop the skills they need to work without direct teacher supervision. At the beginning of academic choice time on Day Twelve, I initiate a role-play on working independently: "Often, during academic choice time, I will be concentrating on some important work with a few students while the rest of you work on your important choice work. You will need to take good care of yourselves so I can do my best teaching for your classmates. I'm going to pretend that I'm a student and I've decided to draw for my choice time." I get a piece of paper and some crayons, go to a table and pretend to draw, then stop and look around the room.

"I just finished a drawing and I don't know what to do next. I think, 'I'll ask the teacher!' but then I see the teacher is busy working on book bags with some kids. What can I do that will take care of what I need without interrupting my teacher?" I take two or three ideas from the students and list them on chart paper.

"You could get more paper and make a new drawing."

"You could see if someone at the table wanted help with their drawing."

"You could ask the other people at your table for ideas what to do."

I choose one of the children's ideas and act it out. After a discussion of how I decided to handle the situation, two or three student volunteers act out the scenario choosing one of the other suggestions on the chart. The role-play helps the class to think more consciously about their choices and decisions in regard to independent work. As they go to choice time, I observe carefully in order to notice and encourage independent behaviors. Many of these behaviors will have already been modeled and practiced during the first two weeks of school.

"Your quiet voices are helping our choice period work well."

"You're putting the markers where everyone can share them, Jesse."

"I see that you showed Erika where we keep the drawing paper, Timmy."

Paradoxical groups

Academics

On the following day, I begin to work with paradoxical groups (see overview for this chapter for a description of "the paradox" teaching strategy). The children continue to practice independent work skills, and I continue to observe, notice, encourage, remind, and redirect them, while at the same time appearing to concentrate on teaching small groups of four or five students.

Today, the small groups are working on making book bags. The book bags are inexpensive cloth tote bags that the children decorate with fabric markers. They will be used each night to carry a book home for students to read to or with parents, then brought back to school the next morning. This will be nightly homework.

With each group, I spend a little time modeling how to use fabric markers and helping the children generate ideas for ways to decorate the bags while practicing on cloth scraps. Most of the time, however, the children draw and color on their own. My attention is free to survey the activities of the rest of the class and provide feedback to them, while appearing to be "busy" with my group. I use this strategy to prepare the class for the upcoming times when I will truly need to concentrate all my attention on instruction of a small group while the rest of the students apply themselves to independent tasks.

Math program

The math program continues with whole-group counting and grouping activities with Unifix® cubes, but now I begin to conduct brief student assessments with individuals while the class works. This helps me get to know children's individual math skills and concepts better, which will aid me in planning the math curriculum for the rest of the year.

Spider science

Science work with spiders provides more opportunities to work outdoors this week while the weather is still good. While we look for spiders around the school grounds, students are also practicing field trip behavior—how to abide by the class rules and concentrate on school work when outside the actual classroom. Before our first excursion, we will talk about ways that we follow our class rules on a field trip.

Since we are still on school grounds, it is easy to stop the action and regroup if behaviors are problematic. Often children find it difficult to generalize rules and expectations beyond the setting in which they have been taught. Field trips on school grounds build upon behaviors practiced during outside games and extend them to more traditionally academic activities.

Along with practice in "outdoor school" and careful, respectful interaction with nature, science lessons this week provide plenty of opportunities to observe spiders carefully and to practice recording and sharing those observations. While learning about spiders, the children are also learning important scientific processes.

Language arts

Reading activities continue at Morning Meeting, quiet time, and story time. During language arts time, the children draw and write about the topic they know best—themselves! Self-portraits begin with the children using mirrors to observe and draw themselves. Art teachers are a great help with lessons on drawing faces.

Once children have drawn a "portrait" of themselves, they spend several days completing a series of worksheets in which they share information about themselves. These eventually become pages in the child's "self-portrait book." The pages include writings and drawings on topics such as the following:

- "If I were an animal, I'd be a ____________."
- "My favorite meal in the whole world is ____________, ____________, ____________, and ____________ for dessert."
- "These are the people in my family: ______________________________ ____."

Once the books are complete, children proudly share them with the class, and they are added to the classroom library, where they can be read and reread. They are also wonderful pieces of student work to share at the first parent meeting or conference. While children learn about the power, fun, and skills of writing, they also learn more about themselves and each other. The curriculum enhances our community, and our community enhances the curriculum.

Day Eleven

8:15 Arrival and morning chart

8:30 Morning Meeting: teach activity—"Coseeki"

9:00 Academic choice/have-tos: three-quarters of the class works on choice while I work with the rest of the class as a small group to introduce handwriting workbooks

9:30 Academic choice/have-tos: children move to a new choice while I begin handwriting workbooks with another small group

10:00 Outside: group initiative

10:30 Language arts: fifteen-minute spelling lesson, silent reading, log writing

11:30 Outside: whole-group cooperative game

12:00 Lunch

12:30 Quiet time

12:50 Read-aloud: read *Alexander and the Terrible, Horrible, No Good, Very Bad Day* by Judith Viorst as an introduction to logical consequences

1:15 Math: whole group with "Investigations"

2:00 Theme: guided discovery of research books in room (dictionaries, encyclopedias)

2:45 Cleanup and closing circle

3:00 Dismissal

Day Twelve

8:15 Arrival and morning chart

9:00 Morning Meeting: all four components are now in place

9:30 Academic choice/have-tos

10:00 Academic choice/have-tos: similar to yesterday, begin the handwriting workbooks with the final two small groups while the rest of the class works at choice activities

10:30 Writing time: pair-share, then write about times you broke the rules

10:45 Language arts: reading and log writing, begin individual conferences

11:30 Outside: cooperative games

12:00 Lunch

12:30 Meeting: define and brainstorm logical consequences

12:50 Read-aloud

1:15 Math

2:00 Theme: research work with encyclopedias

2:45 Cleanup and closing circle

3:00 Dismissal

Day Thirteen

8:15 Arrival and morning chart

8:30 Morning Meeting: introduce and practice time-out

9:00 Academic choice/have-tos

9:30 Academic choice/have-tos

10:00 Outside: group initiative

10:30 Language arts: spelling, reading, log writing, conferences

11:30 Outside: playground games

12:00 Lunch

12:30 Quiet time

12:50 Read-aloud

1:15 Math

2:00 Theme: guided discovery—library research

2:45 Cleanup and closing circle

3:00 Dismissal

Sample Schedule

Week Three

Middle Grades (3-4)

Day Fourteen

8:15 **Arrival and morning chart**

8:30 **Morning Meeting**

9:00 **Academic choice/have-tos**

9:30 **Academic choice/have-tos**

10:00 **Writing/spelling**

10:40 **Reading and log writing:** conferences

11:30 **Outside:** playground games

12:00 **Lunch**

12:30 **Quiet time**

12:50 **Read-aloud**

1:15 **Math**

2:00 **Theme:** library research on caves

2:45 **Cleanup and closing circle**

3:00 **Dismissal**

Day Fifteen

8:15 **Arrival and morning chart**

8:30 **Morning Meeting**

9:00 **Academic choice/have-tos**

9:30 **Academic choice/have-tos**

10:00 **Outside:** group initiative

10:30 **Language arts**

11:30 **Outside:** cooperative game

12:00 **Lunch**

12:30 **Quiet time**

12:50 **Read-aloud**

1:15 **Theme:** topic choice on what students have learned from this week's research

2:30 **Cleanup and Friday closing circle**

3:00 **Dismissal**

Week Three

MIDDLE GRADES (3-4)

Community Building and Tone Setting

Morning Meeting activities

This week, I introduce an inclusive and lively daily activity into Morning Meeting. With the introduction of this component, group activity, the Morning Meeting format is complete. I make sure that the group activities I select this early in the year are easy to learn and are not likely to spotlight particular strengths or difficulties. Often activities will spring from content we are studying; they need not always be games. This daily ritual will continue to be a powerful initial tone-setter each day, developing and reinforcing a sense of community, thoughtfulness, fun, and participation throughout the rest of the year.

Community Building and Tone Setting

Other community builders

Group initiatives, though not done daily, continue to stimulate thinking, cooperation, and bonds among the children that will carry over into the academic curriculum. This is particularly true of the work done in cooperative groups, which will increase a bit in complexity during theme study this week. The activities and approaches we have tended so carefully and thoroughly for the past two weeks now become the backbone of our days—our work-sharing format, academic choice time, closing circles, recess, lunch, quiet time, and reading aloud. As these procedures become habitual and consume less and less of our conscious attention, they provide powerful and dependable support to the growth of our community and the achievement of its individuals.

Rules and Routines

Role-plays

I use role-plays frequently with this age group to help children anticipate common situations, to prompt them to see situations from different points of view, and to get them to generate strategies that help us apply the rules of our classroom to what might be problematic situations. Role-plays allow us to consider an issue in a nonthreatening way—one step removed from the actual event.

Topics and scripts for the role-plays grow from situations I observe or which I know will surface in our daily life. For example, "Pretend you are jumping rope at recess and it's going really well. You love to jump rope! Then someone comes along, someone who can't turn the rope very well, and wants to join. What could you do?" Or, "Pretend my homework isn't ready. The rules say to be honest; the rules also say to do your best work and be prepared for class. What might I do?"

After describing the scenario, I ask for volunteers to act the parts. In the latter example, students would volunteer to play the unprepared student and the teacher. As the students act out the scenario, I stop the action and ask the class what they notice and how the characters might be feeling. What are some alternatives for how the situation could be handled? How do various suggestions fit or not fit our rules? I list the suggestions on a chart, and we choose a few to act out. I end the role-playing session with a summary. Later, I make sure to notice and comment when I see students using positive strategies "offstage."

Logical consequences

Everybody makes mistakes. As I give the children more independence and responsibility, I need to be prepared with constructive reactions when they inevitably break the rules and I need to clearly communicate my intentions to them. I begin that process this week while the independence I give the children is still quite limited and tightly supervised.

"When we do everything correctly, we are showing mastery," I tell them. "When we make mistakes, we have opportunities to learn." I refer to mistakes as noble, because in order to make them, we must take risks. It takes courage to step into an area in which we are not sure we will succeed and to try anyway. If we are to learn and grow, we must be willing to take these risks and make the inevitable mistakes. We do, however, need to learn from our mistakes. A mistake that is not fixed remains, and may lead to more and more problems.

I tell students that, in our class, I use logical consequences to help children learn and grow by fixing mistakes when they make them. I emphasize that we all have good days and bad days; sometimes we make good decisions and sometimes bad ones. Everyone makes mistakes, and doing so carries no shame in this classroom. In fact, shame and guilt make us defensive and can shut down opportunities to grow and learn. Seeing our mistakes as poor choices made in the context of basically good intentions takes away the onus of shame and lets us learn.

This is true whether the mistake involves calculations for 17 + 8, or what to say to a classmate who has just shoved a student out of line. Sometimes I share a story of myself as a child—about a time when I broke the rules, my accompanying feelings, and how I eventually, with great trepidation, made amends.

Rules and Routines

This week, I plan to teach this same idea with a piece of children's literature, *Alexander and the Terrible, Horrible, No Good, Very Bad Day* by Judith Viorst. I read it aloud, then discuss Alexander's day with the children. Students have no trouble relating this story to days in their own lives! The following day's writing time provides a follow-up to this discussion, allowing children to write about occasions when things just seemed to be hard and they ended up making poor decisions. Sharing these times and laughing together about them helps to reinforce the message that making mistakes makes us human, not bad.

Fixing our mistakes

In this context, later the same day, we discuss ways to fix our mistakes. Since our daily schedule is fairly well established now, it is okay, even productive, to occasionally vary it. I use our usual quiet time and read-aloud time to introduce the criteria for logical consequences: they are related, respectful, and reasonable. As a whole group we brainstorm possible "fixes" for various mistaken behaviors. I let the children know that when they are not in good control of themselves, I will take control for them and make decisions about what logical consequence might be helpful.

In the weeks ahead, I will introduce the procedure for "apology of action" in which the misbehaving child follows a format for setting her/his own logical consequence in some situations.

Time-out

By Wednesday morning, the group will be ready to learn about time-out or, as my students and I call it at this grade level, "take a break." This is a strategy I find important in the successful use of logical consequences. I use it when a child is disrupting a group or needs to regain self-control in order to follow the rules of the room.

As with other discussions of reactive discipline measures, I take care to establish the idea that telling a child to take a break from the action in which a misbehavior is occurring is not intended to be punitive but helpful. It is a time to take a few breaths, relax, calm down, and gain self-control.

We model responsible and helpful ways for a student to follow the directive to "take a break." These include going and coming back calmly, sharing with the teacher later if one feels confused or wronged, and strategies for getting oneself in better control while at the "take a break" spot. We also discuss responsible and helpful ways for me to give the directive. These include using a quiet and respectful voice, checking in with the student later if needed, and welcoming the child back into the group.

Once these procedures seem clear to the children, we have some fun acting out ways I might issue the directive that would feel punitive rather than respectful, and ways they could choose to follow it that would not be helpful. At a time when nobody is really breaking any rules, we can laugh together over all the ways we can "blow it." At the same time, my point about the importance of the way we use "take a break" is reinforced, and expectations both for myself and for the children are made quite clear.

Academics

Settling into a routine

The academic curriculum begins to settle into a routine this week. Language arts, math, and theme work occur at predictable times. Children who receive special services remain with the class for now even if they will eventually do some of their work in a different setting. Efforts to build an inclusive community, a sense of individual significance, and clear expectations for routines and behavior are often even more essential to the success of students with special needs than to others.

Fortunately, the nature of the academic curriculum these first weeks makes it possible for all the children not just to cope but to succeed. Specialist teachers, rather than taking children out of the classroom during these first few weeks, come into the classroom during the time they would be working with children, and participate in the ongoing work of the classroom, often enriching our work with their particular expertise. Specialists benefit from the chance to observe the academic and social skills of students in the context of the home classroom, and they get to see how our classroom works. This information is valuable later as they work with the children on their own.

Academics

Reading

The curriculum remains open to a wide range of learners and possible outcomes and products as we continue to focus on work habits and expectations. Having students read independently in self-chosen books allows me to stand back and keep an overview of the group's behavior while the children experience important practice in reading. Their written log entries give me insight into each child's reading ability, comprehension, and ability to summarize and express ideas in writing. In addition, I begin to conference with individuals this week, listening to students read, asking questions, and sharing enjoyment of books together. The nature of these first conferences is simple enough that I can conduct them while still keeping a watchful eye on the rest of the class.

Paradoxical groups

Central to my planning for the third week of school is the creation of "the paradox" (see overview for this chapter for a description of "the paradox" teaching strategy). While children work on familiar independent activities established in the first two weeks, I begin to work with individuals or small groups. During choice time, for example, the children whom I have assigned to work with me in a small group have a "have-to" for that period, while the rest may choose what they will do within the parameters of academic choice options. Though eventually I will simply call this a work period, I introduce it as a choice/have-to time.

As I work with a small group or individual, I appear to leave those children who are not working directly with me on their own. However, I have chosen an activity for the small group that does not require a great deal of direct instruction, so that I can actually continue to closely observe the independent workers who are not in the small group. While they enjoy a sense of "flying" on their own, I am still flying alongside them, ready to encourage or redirect as needed. Their initial independent flights are assured reasonable success, and habits of responsibility and independence grow.

Handwriting instruction

I find handwriting instruction suited to this time period because the *D'Nealian Handwriting* workbooks that I use build in a certain amount of structure and guidance (see references for a full citation). Also, the books begin with a review of manuscript letters with which children in third- and fourth-grade classes are familiar. The focus of new learning can then be on working independently while the teacher is working with a small group.

Day Eleven

8:30 Arrival and morning chart

8:45 Morning Meeting: develop meeting rules during sharing and activity time

9:15 Social studies: introduce logical consequences

10:00 Group initiative: "Platform" (round two)

10:45 Math: graphing unit—individuals will plan what information they want to gather and begin to gather it

11:30 Outside: teach soccer

12:00 Lunch

12:30 Lunch sharing

1:00 Read-aloud

1:40 Language arts: continue independent reading projects

2:30 Cleanup and journal writing

2:50 Closing circle

3:00 Dismissal

Day Twelve

8:30 Arrival and morning chart

8:45 Morning Meeting

Greeting: teach group juggling

9:15 Social studies

Sharing of final draft interviews from last week

Homework: Find and bring in the oldest artifact in your home that you are allowed to bring to school and find out how your family came to own it.

10:00 Science: guided discovery of batteries, bulbs, and wires

10:45 Math: graphing unit—complete data collection and begin rough draft bar graphs

11:30 Outside: teach kickball

12:00 Lunch

12:30 Lunch sharing

12:40 Read-aloud

1:00 Language arts: meet with a small group to work in spelling books while the rest of the class works on independent projects

1:45 Language arts: meet with another small group

2:30 Cleanup and journal writing

2:50 Closing circle

3:00 Dismissal

Day Thirteen

8:30 Arrival and morning chart

8:45 Morning Meeting

9:15 Social studies

Pair-share old artifact and accompanying stories

Brainstorm ways to represent the information

Begin topic choice sequence on the stories of the artifacts

10:00 Science: proceed with study of batteries and bulbs

10:45 Math: graphing unit—complete final draft graphs

11:30 Outside: teach basketball

12:00 Lunch

12:30 Lunch check-in

12:40 Read-aloud

1:00 Language arts: work with a small group in spelling workbooks

2:00 Group initiative: "Jelly Roll"

2:45 Cleanup and journal writing

3:00 Dismissal

Sample Schedule

Week Three

Upper Grades (5–6)

Day Fourteen

8:30 Arrival and morning chart

8:45 Morning Meeting: introduce new greeting—"Spider Web"

9:15 Social studies

Continue topic choice work

Share choice work

10:00 Science: batteries and bulbs unit

10:45 Math: graphing unit—work with a small group to represent their graphs to each other while the rest of the class plays math games

11:30 Outside: introduce playground activities

12:00 Lunch

12:30 Generate rules for recess

1:00 Language arts: same as Day Thirteen

2:00 Group initiative: complete "Jelly Roll" or begin new initiative

2:45 Cleanup and journal writing

3:00 Dismissal

Day Fifteen

8:30 Arrival and morning chart

8:45 Morning Meeting

9:15 Social studies: work-sharing—share finished choice work projects

10:00 Science: batteries and bulbs unit

10:45 Math: meet with a small group to represent their graphs while rest of class plays math games

11:30 Outside: introduce "outside choice"

12:00 Lunch

12:30 Lunch and outside time check-in

12:40 Read-aloud

1:00 Language arts: meet with any remaining small group to work in spelling books while rest of class works on independent reading projects

2:30 Cleanup and appreciation circle

3:00 Dismissal

Week Three

UPPER GRADES (5–6)

Community Building and Tone Setting

Community Building and Tone Setting

Morning Meeting greetings

The routines of Morning Meeting are now fully under way. I plan to introduce a couple of new greetings during the week. Otherwise, we will continue with the basic "Good Morning" greeting practiced last week. My experience has shown me that fifth- and sixth-graders often prefer this simple and dignified greeting. Its highly ritualized nature is brief, reassuring, and powerful. But I make sure to teach other greetings as well. Sometimes we need a break from routine, and some groups prefer a wide variety of greetings. Over time, each group of students will discover its own preferences.

Sharing also becomes a daily routine. Beginning this week, I simply call on children who raise their hands to share, then check their names off on a class list. When everyone on the list who wants to share has had a turn, we begin again with a fresh list (perhaps the next week). I allow for one "urgent" sharing a day from someone who might have already had a turn in the week, but wants very much to tell the class about some important, current event in her/his life. This might include the outcome of an anticipated event reported earlier ("My sister had the baby. It's a girl!") or it might be new ("Our car broke down on the way to school!"). My goal is for sharing time to develop into a time of spontaneous and fun dialogue together, within the safety of a predictable structure.

The appreciation circle

The appreciation circle also gains more spontaneity this week. I now allow children to give one or two "appreciations" to classmates of their choice in addition to the one whose name they drew. In this way, I know everyone in the class will be acknowledged at least once, but other sincere recognition has a forum as well.

Group initiatives

The group initiatives this week become more complex and require more time to complete and discuss. They happen regularly, but not daily, as we begin to settle into the schedule we will follow the rest of the year. On Day Eleven, we complete the "Platform" exercise begun on Day Ten. On Days Thirteen and Fourteen, I allot two 45-minute periods in the afternoon to work on the "Jelly Roll." The object of this initiative is to transport the entire group over an area covered with an imaginary poisonous jelly substance using only four large industrial paper tubes, which may touch the jelly, and a two-inch by ten-inch by twelve-foot board, which may not touch the jelly. Solving the problem requires a high level of communication and cooperation—not to mention creativity!

Once the students are outside and the initiative begins, I step in only to freeze the action and regroup if behavior and frustration levels appear counterproductive or harmful. If the group seems a long way from completing the task on the second day, we'll begin the session indoors, debriefing and developing a plan with my facilitation. This should allow them to finish successfully. I set aside two 45-minute sessions for a new initiative problem next week, so the children can enjoy and reinforce the skills and strategies developed through solving this initiative.

Outdoor games

Over the last two weeks, students have learned a repertoire of cooperative games which will be offered as outdoor choices in the future. Now we are ready to tackle the more difficult competitive team games. This is instructional time—not downtime—because as far as both the physical and the social-emotional curricula are concerned, recess is one of the most important times of day for learning.

As mentioned earlier, this instruction in outdoor play is best done with the physical education teacher, or with the person who will be supervising recess. If the physical education teacher is not available, however, I find it very worth my time and energy to spend the first few weeks of school "teaching recess" in collaboration with the recess supervisor. Later, there will be much less conflict and trauma among the students as they return to class from recess. This carries over into higher productivity and learning, and enables the group to enjoy greater camaraderie.

Before children truly have a choice about what they will do during recess, they must each have an opportunity to learn the various games they will choose among. They also must have thought about and practiced ways to play competitive games in a way that's friendly and fun for all. Otherwise, many recess activities will be comfortable only for those children who are already adept at them, and important opportunities for learning and physical education will be lost. Therefore, I teach the popular recess games of soccer, kickball, and basketball to the entire class before opening some recess times to choices made by the children. I also spend one outside time in a guided discovery of playground equipment, such as swings and slides. During this week, the class is learning and practicing the rules for how we play games and use equipment at our school.

We will also discuss and role-play ways to follow the class rules when conflicts and frustrations arise during the game. We will role-play situations such as what to do when someone wants to join a game already in progress, or how to follow class rules when a teammate makes a poor play in the game and "costs" his/her team the game.

Community Building and Tone Setting

Rules and Routines

Rules and Routines

Conversations about applying the rules

As the students discuss and practice safe, friendly ways to play these school-yard games, they are applying the newly created classroom rules to recess time in very concrete ways. Each day brings new opportunities for discussion of our rules. I frequently begin these conversations with a question:

"If our rule says that we'll be safe, what are some things we can do to follow the rule as we play kickball?"

"If we have agreed to treat each other with respect, how will that look as we play soccer?"

"What does our rule about taking care of the environment have to do with what we do on the playground equipment?"

Role-playing

I use role-plays regularly to help students rehearse ways to react to the many potential problem situations that will arise during the school day. Role-plays allow us to consider a problem in a nonthreatening way—one step removed from the actual event.

I might say, for example, "Let's imagine that I'm about to have a turn to kick in a kickball game, but the person before me has just struck our team's third out and now I'll miss my turn. I feel mad at the person who just struck out! But our rule says we'll be nice to each other. What could I do that would follow our rule?" The group thinks together about constructive ways to handle this situation, which students then act out.

I end each role-playing session with a summary and later make sure I notice and comment when I see students using positive strategies "offstage" (see Key Terms for a detailed example of a role-play).

Making the rules come alive

One of the central goals of this week is to make the rules we worked hard to create come alive in daily practice. I frequently refer to the rules in the context of daily activities and lessons, and provide opportunities for the children to share their ideas of behaviors that follow the rules and then to practice those behaviors.

I have often heard teachers of eleven- and twelve-year-olds express doubt that such modeling, role-playing, and conscious practice is necessary or even acceptable to these students. However, I find that concrete application of abstract rules to specific situations remains crucial to establishing positive behavioral guidelines, even with eleven- and twelve-year-olds. Because the approach invites student input about what behaviors "follow our rules," I find that older children will usually become highly involved in the process. They also love to be actors in the role-plays!

Keeping discussions "real"

It is critical, however, that the discussions are allowed to be "real." If I ask questions such as the ones suggested above, I must be willing to accept any sincere and respectful responses as legitimate contributions to the conversation. Most fifth- and sixth-graders are quick to spot a phony question—one whose "correct" answer the teacher has already decided—and resent it. They may act out their resentment with silly or unreasonable responses, and the discussion will be useless at best, possibly even out of control and counterproductive.

In order for these discussions to be engaging and effective for students, teachers themselves must find the questions engaging and provocative. We must trust our students' ability and willingness to engage in sincere discussion and be open to their thinking on the subject. And we must trust our own ability to facilitate these discussions to ends that are respectful of all involved, including ourselves. When these conditions are in place, such conversations encourage high standards for our students' thinking.

Address a *few* key issues

Opportunities to discuss, practice, and role-play behaviors that follow the rules arise continually. Obviously, we cannot address them all in one week. There would be no time for anything else, and the students would be too overwhelmed with information and fatigued by the process to gain much. I remind myself often that I will have an entire year with these children, and plenty of juicy situations will present themselves for our consideration and interpretation. For this week, I will address a few key issues and times of day: recess, lunch, transition times, and Morning Meeting.

By the end of the week, we will have established a subset of more specific behavioral rules for recess, lunch, and Morning Meeting. To do this, we use an abbreviated version of the format we used to make the classroom rules.

Rules and Routines

Logical Consequences

These sets of rules for specific situations will often serve as "shorthand" reminders. "Meeting rules, please," is more efficient and respectful than "Nicky, put your binder down," and "Lucy and Caitlin, stop whispering." It is more specific in its allusion to specific behaviors than a general "Pay attention, class."

These rules for specific situations are also useful as reference points when checking in on how lunch and/or recess went. Often, I can simply ask at check-in time, "On a scale of one to ten, how did you do at following the rules for lunch (or recess)?" Children simply give a number and a reason for giving it.

Logical Consequences

Introducing logical consequences

I introduce logical consequences to fifth- and sixth-graders in a matter-of-fact manner by sharing my philosophy of discipline. "I want everyone in our room to feel okay about making mistakes," I might say, "but when you make mistakes, I do expect you to fix them. That is how we learn, whether we are fixing mistakes in math or mistakes in how we treat ourselves or each other. Often we manage to fix our own mistakes, and that's great! But sometimes, that is just more than we can do. We might feel upset, and it's very hard to have enough self-control to stop ourselves and fix our mistakes when we are upset. When that happens, we need help, and at those times I will tell you what you need to do. I will take you out of a situation if you are not making helpful choices about your behavior, so you can cool down for a bit before you make amends. What you need to do to make amends or fix your mistakes is called the logical consequence. Once you've fixed the mistake with a logical consequence, we can let go of the problem and move on."

I teach students this age the three categories of logical consequences:

1. *Making reparations: "You break it—you fix it"*
2. *Mishandling responsibility—more limits set*
3. *Jeopardizing the group safety or functioning (in physical or emotional ways)—time-out from the group or activity*

I want the students to have an idea of the thinking I do when I determine a consequence for misbehavior and some guidelines for doing so on their own.

In order to give time-out dignity when many have experienced it only as indignity, I try to take away negative connotations associated with it by spending a lot of time introducing it. I compare it to time-out in a basketball game, and I discuss ways adults give themselves time-outs when they are overwhelmed with emotion and on the verge of disrespectful behavior. Students enjoy an honest discussion of the pros and cons of time-out and how we can use it in a helpful rather than hurtful way.

I usually ask students to brainstorm ideas for what we can call it. I've heard many ideas from "taking a vacation," "cooling out," or "taking a break," to "the elevator" (elevators are quiet and away from the action, but they get you where you want to go). I also share important considerations in choosing a time-out place in the room and listen to students' ideas for its placement. I find students quite thoughtful about these questions, and we actually have fun setting up time-out.

The part students often enjoy the most comes after a few students have demonstrated helpful ways to go to the time-out place. A few lucky volunteers then get to take turns demonstrating some of the unhelpful ways to go to time-out! Students love to act out the kid who argues, stomps away, and/or makes faces. While we laugh at these antics when they are removed from a real problem situation, important points are made: we are all aware of these behaviors; they are nothing new; and they do not help.

Academics

Science

Science begins with a guided discovery of batteries, bulbs, and wires—an important part of our first unit on electricity. Students explore the possibilities of these materials, solve problems requiring their use, and do research to find answers to student-generated questions arising from this work. I start with this unit because it provides opportunities to use group cooperation and problem-solving strategies, upon which we have been working intensively during the group initiatives. It also provides more practice working with and caring for materials and working independently in small groups. As with other curricula used during the first six weeks of school, children with a wide range of skill and knowledge levels participate successfully.

Academics

Social studies

This week, our social studies work brings an initial experience with choosing a project. The content—stories about an old family artifact—comes from the students' personal experience. New information comes from learning the procedures and sequences of the choice format and from the learning that occurs as students share their stories with each other. Here again, the content is accessible to every learner in the class, and all can participate successfully. Meanwhile, students are practicing skills important to social scientists—the study of artifacts and the research and documentation of the stories that go with them.

Math and language arts

Math and language arts are fairly well established now. The whole group is accustomed to working independently on projects and games while I circulate, interacting informally with students and overseeing behavior. Now, during these times I begin "the paradox," in which I appear to the children to focus on a small group for instruction while the remainder of the class works independently.

For example, I might facilitate small groups as they present their math graphs to each other, while the rest of the class plays math games. Since the small group is presenting work already completed, I do not need to offer new instruction. While attending to the presenting and giving some direction to the small group, I am also able to observe and give feedback to the independent workers.

Similarly, the work with spelling books during language arts allows me to look at the spelling abilities of a small group. However, since the workbooks provide guidelines for the activities, I am able to spend lots of this time making sure that the children working on independent reading projects are appropriately on task. The students are learning that even when my attention is divided, the rules remain in place and they are expected to follow them. We are preparing for the upcoming time when I will truly focus my attention on instruction with small groups and/or individuals in the midst of the larger group.

MARCH

Weeks Four to Six

CHAPTER FOUR

During an initial phase which usually takes the first three weeks of the school year, many routines, procedures, and concepts are introduced and established. The second three-week phase is a time of transition between the carefully crafted introductions of the beginning of the year and the independence which comes when the classroom is in "full swing."

The introductory phase may take longer than three weeks. Below are some benchmarks that will help you decide when your students are ready to move into the second phase. These benchmarks refer to students' independent accomplishment of the daily routines, to the overall tone and sense of community, and to the commencement of study in regular academic subject areas.

You will notice that the descriptions of these benchmarks use phrases like "most children" and "most of the time." Everyone is entitled to lapses now and then. For some children, remembering the routines and behaving consistently with appropriate self-control will take far more than a few weeks of intensive focus. When deciding whether students are ready for more responsibility, we are seeking a sense of the usual—what most of the students are doing much of the time.

The Benchmarks

- **Students should be competent at the basic practices and procedures of the room.** Most children, most of the time, line up quickly and calmly and move through the hallways quietly and safely. They use established bathroom procedures with little disruption of ongoing classroom activities. During morning arrival and afternoon dismissal, they need few, if any, reminders about details such as turning in homework, storing or retrieving their backpacks, and doing their cleanup jobs. Students efficiently locate, productively use, and responsibly care for common classroom supplies, such as markers, scissors, staplers, and books.

- **Children's behavior reflects a sense of the class as a community, with a tone and ethos of mutual respect, order, and belonging.** Students listen to one another and offer respectful questions, comments, and ideas to classmates and teachers during most meetings and lessons. Friendships have increased since the first day of school, and children enjoy a friendly, calm lunchtime and recess on most days. Children can name classroom rules and, with their teacher's guidance, demonstrate specific actions that follow the rules in different situations. They are familiar with the concept of logical consequences, including the rationale and goals for using them, and have experienced logical consequences established by teachers.
- **All regular academic subject areas have been introduced in the first weeks, and now the regular daily schedule is in effect.** Specialists work with students as they will for the rest of the year, joining the room for Morning Meetings and other activities as often as possible.

Overview

During Weeks Four, Five, and Six, the curriculum moves slowly and steadily beyond the introductions of the first phase of the year toward more complex roles and responsibilities for students. The eventual expectation is that all students will be engaged in challenging, personally satisfying academic work much of the time in a friendly, respectful community of learners. The content of the curriculum builds bridges between the students' previous knowledge and experiences and the new information to be gained this year. It also continues to build bridges among class members.

The best units of study during this time fulfill a number of criteria. They integrate social and academic skills. They begin with students' current knowledge and allow for direct, shared experiences as a basis for building additional knowledge. Applicable to a range of skill levels, they focus on topics that are fundamentally compelling to the age group, and they allow for in-depth exploration of a relatively narrow topic.

When the group seems ready, taking them beyond school walls in order to learn is important. Such "field work" allows the group to participate in challenges that are similar to those of group initiatives and are an essential part of the learning process. The games, the group initiatives, the cooperative and trust-building activities support and merge with the academic curriculum, helping students to care deeply, take risks, cooperate, and work hard toward goals.

Whether you teach through integrated thematic units, separate subject areas, or a combination of the two, topics and processes of study should be carefully chosen for this time. They will play an important role in the degree to which students internalize the lessons of the first weeks and apply them throughout the rest of the year.

With the ongoing daily schedule in place, we can now focus on establishing as independent habits the work and social behaviors taught in the first three weeks. We use two basic approaches to help us do this:

Weeks Four to Six

1. **Provide more coached practice while giving students ever-increasing degrees of independence and responsibility.** Under the watchful and encouraging eye of the teacher, regular practice of whole-group, small-group, and independent activities continues in these weeks. As students seem ready, we turn more and more responsibilities over to them.
2. **Provide a variety of opportunities (such as conflict resolution protocols or Class Meeting) for students to internalize behavioral expectations by applying their own understandings to social situations.** We choose among several new strategies—self-rating based upon student-generated criteria, apology of action, Class Meeting, and conflict resolution methods—that incorporate and build upon strategies used in the introductory weeks. These strategies help to build understandings and skills that allow students to become increasingly independent. The high degree of external control necessary during the first few weeks is now diminished and replaced with an increasing degree of internal motivation and self-control.

It is important to note that teachers choose among several strategies to introduce next, after considering which strategies best fit their teaching style and their particular class. They teach only one strategy at a time and do not introduce new ones until prior ones are familiar and students are routinely, successfully using them.

Because the strategies named in this chapter work at all elementary grades, we have not divided this chapter by grade level. However, teachers will need to apply their knowledge of their students' development and the needs of particular groups to adapt the language and complexity of the strategies to their classes. For example, we would wait to introduce Class Meetings to primary-grade children (K–2) until much later than the fourth week of school, and these meetings must be short and limited to a single topic.

Continuing to give students opportunities to reflect, discuss, and problem-solve allows them to construct an understanding of why and how certain behaviors work better than others, and to increase their repertoire of positive responses to difficult situations. When added to the clearly delineated routines and expectations of the first weeks, students' increased understanding helps them to work and play productively with ever-increasing independence.

Goals for Weeks Four to Six

- **Most children work independently while the teacher focuses on individuals or small groups.**
- **Children work together productively and kindly in both teacher- and child-formed groups.**
- **Students are familiar with a large number of tools and resources for learning and expressing learning, and locate and use them independently and constructively.**
- **Children show that they are beginning to internalize classroom rules by generating and discussing strategies for following the rules independently in problematic situations.**
- **All children experience logical consequences for misbehaviors.**
- **Students show an understanding of the role of logical consequences by contributing ideas for their use during Class Meetings, independent conflict resolution, and apology of action.**
- **Children become increasingly independent in following classroom routines by taking responsibility for leading them and by following the lead of classmates.**

Goals for Weeks Four to Six

Strategies for Working on the Goals of Weeks Four to Six

Strategy: Stop and Think Aloud

During these weeks, we regularly stop lessons, recesses, transitions, and routines to ask students to think aloud about how to proceed. We elicit children's plans for following procedures established in the first weeks, refreshing their memories and prompting them to elaborate upon these procedures. We ask questions such as "What will you do to get ready for recess? Reading group? Dismissal?" Or, after preparation and a couple of trips to the library, "When we get to the library today to work on our research, what will you do?"

Strategies

This process of thinking aloud allows children to learn rapidly from others' experience while the teacher listens, watches, and responds with immediate feedback. We also continue to ask children to reflect upon what they did well and not so well after a work or social time.

Strategy in Action

Morning Meeting ends with a round of applause celebrating the children's identification and correction of all ten misspelled words in the morning message. "I can see that your brains are sharp today!" I announce proudly. " I'm looking forward to seeing what ideas you have for writing. When I dismiss you, get set up for writing time. I'll work with group B on journals while the rest of you work independently on writing. Let's think together. How will you get ready for independent writing?"

"We need to get our writing folders and two pencils in case one breaks," Matteo offers.

"Yes, Matteo, your pencil broke on you yesterday, didn't it? Thanks for sharing your plan for dealing with that problem today," I respond. "Any other good ideas for getting ready? What if you get stuck? I won't be able to help you, because I'll be busy with the journal group."

"If you might need some ideas, you could bring a book or two to look at," Travis suggests. "And once, I asked someone at my table for help, and he told me an idea."

Kira adds, "Bring your spelling dictionary. I used mine a lot yesterday."

"Okay. Sounds like you have some helpful ideas," I say. "When I say 'now,' I'm going to sit back and watch you all do your best job yet of getting ready for writing. How long do you think it should take?"

"Three minutes!" claim several students.

"No, two, two!" shouts an enthusiastic Gordon, who does, in fact, do everything in

a third less time than his classmates, moving through school in permanent overdrive.

"Wow! Two? Wouldn't that be great?" I respond. "Let's go for three minutes today, and if we make it, we'll see if most of us want to go for two tomorrow. Okay," I pause, signaling the coming transition, "now."

The children rise and begin to collect writing supplies, sharpen pencils, get drinks, and settle in at tables.

"Good thinking," I nod as Emmy hangs her bathroom tag and looks at me. "I see several of you are finding books to bring with you," I remark. "This class is certainly showing some careful planning for writing time. We've taken two minutes so far."

There is a final urgent scurry to grab one last pencil, dig a notebook from beneath a pile of papers, and fall into a seat. At the last second, Emmy returns from the bathroom, sliding triumphantly into her seat.

"You did it!" I announce. "Three minutes." I turn to my small group and begin. "Let's read the worksheet together and see what you'll be writing about yourselves today."

Weeks Four to Six

Strategy: Continue "Paradoxical" Group Work

As we did in Week Three, we continue to plan lessons for small groups so the rest of the class can practice responsible independence. Despite appearances, our primary job during these times is to observe and coach the "independent" workers while working with the small group on some task that does not take most of our attention and energy.

While the students work hard at practicing independent work habits, the teacher works to ensure students' success through diligent observation and attention to detail. We carefully choose words to communicate our observations as useful feedback for the children. We notice positive behaviors and use reminders and redirection as soon as we see students begin to stray from the carefully established expectations for independent work times. We also notice and encourage the work of the group with whom we sit.

Very slowly and gradually over the next weeks, as we note good independent work habits solidifying, we turn more of our attention to the small group, planning work for them that will require more teacher input.

Strategy in Action

As the writing time proceeds, the small group uses the guidelines I've provided to write in their journals, leaving me free to survey the room frequently.

"Jasmine, what can you do so you won't need to stop work and go to the pencil sharpener again before we are done with writing time?"

"Alton, once you're seated, you stay seated."

"I see that some of you are helping each other with ideas for your writing."

"You are managing to keep your voices soft today. It's easy to concentrate."

I end the work time about five minutes early, announcing, "I saw a lot of writing happening in the last half hour. The journal writing group was able to complete their assignment. Let's share some thoughts about what we did to make this writing time productive."

"Most of us stayed in our same seats once we sat down," Marcus claims with lifted chin and challenging eyes. Staying in his seat is an ongoing challenge for Marcus, and his sharing is as much a request for recognition as a statement of fact.

"Most of you certainly did!" I grin at Marcus warmly. "That really helped a lot."

"When Alisha didn't know what to do next, I helped her by giving her some ideas," Chantell shares. Alisha nods in agreement.

"I remembered to get enough paper this time," Andrew chuckles.

Strategies

"Great! You are really getting good at helping each other and thinking ahead," I conclude. "Now it's time to get your books for reading. Let's see how long it takes until we are all settled and ready to read. I'll dismiss you by tables." I take a deep breath and prepare to watch and coach again.

Strategy: Turning More Over to Students

As the weeks pass and students demonstrate increasing responsibility and caring, many routine responsibilities and decisions are slowly turned over to them. The predictable rituals of Morning Meeting provide one such opportunity. As children become familiar with each component and the group builds a common repertoire of greetings, sharing topics, and activities, students can lead the group.

Some teachers designate a different child to select activities for some or all components each day or each week. That child is responsible (after a quick check-in with the teacher) for announcing the activity and calling on classmates to participate. Teachers, of course, still guide the meeting, setting limits when needed, and demonstrating the importance of Morning Meeting and the validity of student leadership in daily classroom life through their presence and participation.

Some teachers enlist student leadership for some days of the week, while maintaining their own leadership on other days. Students might run meetings on Tuesdays and Thursdays, for example, or on Tuesdays, Wednesdays, and Thursdays. This gives the teacher the flexibility to introduce new activities and greetings or break routine with a discussion of some current event or classroom issue as needed. Mondays and Fridays can be particularly important times for using this option.

Other daily routines for which children of all ages may take responsibility (with varying degrees of independence) include attendance-taking and reporting to the office, lunch counts, leading the Pledge of Allegiance, running errands, or collecting book club orders.

Strategy: Using Logical Consequences

It is important in the very first weeks to make sure that children know the rules of the classroom. In Weeks One and Two, the rules were established. In Week Three, we introduced the concept of logical consequences for breaking rules, taking time to discuss, model, problem-solve, and role-play. Now teachers must use logical consequences—consistently, quickly, compassionately, and without apology. It is another kind of feedback for students as they make mistakes and try out behaviors in their quest to ascertain that school is a safe and predictable place in which they can take risks and learn.

Because we work hard to make consequences for misbehavior respectful and constructive rather than punitive, we do not hesitate to use them when needed. Logical consequences guide children while they practice—and test—the expectations for behavior. Applying logical consequences reinforces the boundaries of appropriate behavior in children's minds.

The following examples illustrate using different types of logical consequences: making reparations, limiting of choices, and time-out.

Making reparations: "You break it—you fix it"

Strategy in Action

The first-graders chatter excitedly as they put away the math supplies and line up for outside games. Michael, Shawn, and Andre begin to tussle playfully by the door while they wait for their classmates to join them. I station myself in the doorway directly in front of the frolicking threesome and raise my hand in the signal for quiet and attention. As the students around them begin to quiet their voices and bodies and raise their hands too, Michael, Andre, and Shawn look around at me and then they, too, settle into stillness and raise their hands.

"Let's go" is all I say. Michael leads the line toward the front door. As I watch, he rounds the corner, breaking into a run. Shawn and Andre join him. Michael skids over a freshly painted poster that a group of fifth-graders left outside their door to dry in the hall. The other two knock several jackets off coat hooks in an attempt to avoid stepping on the poster. Before I can stop them, the threesome slams sideways into the front door, hit the release bar, and charge outside yelling, "Yea!"

I stay with the rest of the group until they, too, are on the playground. Then I calmly approach Shawn, Michael, and Andre. "I will go back inside with you, so you can fix the coats and poster you messed up. Then I will watch you follow our rules in the hall on your way back outside."

"Awww..." they mutter in disappointment.

"Let's go." I begin walking, and the children follow.

No matter how well children can describe respectful and safe ways to behave, no matter how many times they have successfully practiced, they will sometimes either accidentally or purposely forget established procedures. This happens most when they are excited, discouraged, or tired.

Michael, Andre, and Shawn were excited. The teacher knew this and appreciated their enthusiasm. She also knew that their careless behavior offered an important opportunity to teach them a way to acknowledge and make reparation for mistakes.

Strategies

Because the teacher felt compassion for the children's motivations, she was able to deliver a calm, matter-of-fact response to their loss of self-control. Because the children had practiced doing so successfully many times, the teacher was confident that they knew and could follow the expected behavior for traveling through the halls. Because she was clear that the logical consequence would help them grow as responsible individuals, she felt no need to argue, lecture, or negotiate when the students expressed reluctance to make reparations. And, at least partly, because she did not shame, embarrass, or lecture the children in the face of their misbehavior or subsequent reluctance, they went with her to "fix" their mistakes with minimum resistance.

Reacting to children's misbehavior with logical consequences requires decisive action. We must let children know clearly what they need to do in as few words as possible. When students are in emotional overdrive, as they generally are when "misbehaving," their rational, reasoning selves are not functioning optimally. Words of reason, argument, or persuasion rarely help and can, in fact, intensify resistance. Whether a child is five or thirteen, logical consequences serve their function best when delivered in a calm, even friendly, manner with as few words as possible.

Mishandling responsibility—more limits set

Setting more limits as a logical consequence assumes that children are regularly given choices and the freedom to try handling responsibility at levels appropriate for them. These choices might range from the freedom to choose where to sit in the

Morning Meeting circle to the opportunity to work out of the direct sight of a teacher. Going to the bathroom without having to ask permission or wait to be escorted, or delivering a message to the office are other examples. When students show us that they aren't ready to handle the level of responsibility a situation demands, it is a logical consequence that we set more limits, at least temporarily, to take back more control until, in our judgment, it is time for the children to try again.

Strategy in Action

The sixth-graders are working on book projects. Some students paint, cut, and glue, or construct figures out of clay. Some read to classmates; some write alone or in chattering huddles. I have told the class that they may choose to develop skits, make models, create "newspapers," or make maps to share important aspects of their books. They may also choose any place to work in the room as long as they follow the class rules. Since the book projects require lots of activity and a variety of supplies and collaborations, these choices allow for creativity and efficiency for the young people.

Weeks Four to Six

Jen, Lena, and Caitlin ask, "Can we go in the hall to practice our skits? There's not enough room in here."

"Can you practice quietly enough not to disturb other classes?" I ask.

"Oh yes!" the girls assure me, and they are off, clutching their scripts and props.

Five minutes later, hearing shrieks of laughter in the hall, I lean around the door in time to see that the girls have begun to play a very silly game of "bowling" with their props and some game balls they found in the hall. As I walk into the middle of the game, Jen freezes midthrow, while her companions quickly pick up the "bowling pin" props.

"We're getting right back to work, now, Ms. D. Promise!" Jen smiles winningly and the others nod in agreement.

"Looks to me like practicing in the hall isn't working out so well right now," I observe. "I'll clear a table in the room where you can sit and work for the rest of the period."

"We'll practice quietly out here! Really!"

"We CAN'T practice in the room! It's too crowded. And besides we don't want everyone to see our skits before we perform them! We can be quiet, now!"

I shake my head. "Girls, you broke our agreement. For the rest of today, you'll have to figure out what you CAN do while sitting in the classroom. We'll give this another try tomorrow."

It would certainly be tempting in a situation such as this to allow the girls to try again immediately. After all, the girls really did need to practice to meet their deadline, and they were usually well behaved. Their promises were even a little convincing.

However, project completion was only one of the teacher's goals for these children. Equally important was the practice of increased independence following the guidelines for behavior the group had spent much of Week Two developing. The teacher wanted the girls to know that she really believed that they were capable of abiding by those rules, even when no authority watched, and that she expected them to do so. Letting them try working away from her sight provided not only an opportunity to practice for book projects, but also an opportunity to try out a higher degree of responsibility. When the temptation to "goof off" became too great for the girls, the teacher acted quickly to bring them back into the safety of increased supervision. They would have another chance to take on this responsibility soon. Meanwhile, they needed to know that their teacher would maintain clear, nonnegotiable limits on behavior—without argument or blame—when their own limits wobbled.

Strategies

Time-out

As with other types of logical consequences, the concepts and procedures of time-out have been taught in Week Three. Now it is time to use time-out as a logical consequence when a student's rule-breaking is jeopardizing either the physical or emotional safety of the class, letting students know that the rules we established together really will be honored.

Strategy in Action

"It's time for Morning Meeting! You know what to do. Let's see if we can set up chairs and be ready to start in two minutes," I announce. The third-graders begin to put away pencils, markers, and journals, then scoot chairs to the meeting area just as they have done for the last four weeks. Catching sight of his new best buddy already setting up on the meeting rug, Kris grabs a chair and swings it wildly behind him as he charges through the group at his table to set up beside Tyrone on the meeting rug.

"Take a break, Kris," directs Ms. Oldham.

Strategy in Action

The second-graders take turns sharing the science observations recently completed. "I looked at the bluebird skeleton," says Monique, as she holds up a drawing with notes written beneath it. "I like the way I drew the skull. You can see the eye holes. The wings were hard to draw. I'm ready for questions and comments."

"Wing bones are easy to draw!" shouts Erin in exasperation.

"Rest stop, Erin," says her teacher.

When a child is angry or upset

Sometimes, when students are very angry or upset, time-out procedures serve to allow the rest of the class to proceed with a minimum of disruption. Time-out functions as a temporary reprieve from a complex situation that disrupts the needs of the classroom community for the needs of one member. The complexity of the situation may require more attention and action by the teacher later, but we must have a way of keeping a classroom in control until we can address the problem more fully.

Strategy in Action

Mr. Sayre announces, "Time to get ready for math." It's a subject with which Liz struggles. She continues to sit and read her independent reading book while the rest of the class bustles about, putting away books and gathering math supplies. He gives her a minute, then walks to Liz and comments, "Looks like you're enjoying your book."

"Yeah," Liz mutters avoiding his eyes.

"Right now, however, it's time for math," he states.

"Nope, not for me. I'm not gonna do math today," scowls Liz, still gazing down at her book.

"Math is what is happening in our class right now, Liz. It sounds like you wish you could just skip it. I'd like to hear more about why that is later, when there is time to talk. But right now, you need to get ready for math time."

"No! I won't! Math is stupid!"

"Liz, take a break," he directs.

In this case, the teacher doesn't expect that a time-out will provide a long-term solution that will help Liz come to math group productively. Liz's mother had called Mr. Sayre recently, concerned that Liz has not "been herself lately," and letting him know of some changes at home. There is much in this situation that he needs to explore and consider in order to help Liz. However, he cannot deal with it at this moment. It would mean neglecting his responsibility to the rest of the class. Also, Liz is clearly upset and needs time to calm down before she can share helpful information about her feelings or take in any feedback. She needs a break to get herself in control, and the teacher needs to be able to move ahead and teach the other students.

When a child won't go: the buddy teacher system

Sometimes when intense emotional upset accompanies a child's misbehavior, she/he may refuse the teacher's directive to go to time-out. In the scene discussed above, Liz might very well have refused to go to time-out. For these times, it is important to have a back-up procedure in place, such as a "buddy teacher." It allows both teacher and student to disengage from power struggles and potentially embarrassing or hurtful emotional displays.

Strategy in Action

"Liz, take a break," directs Mr. Sayre.

"No, I won't! You can't make me!" Liz cries.

Mr. Sayre feels his frustration quickly turn to anger. He takes a deep breath and walks away from Liz, observing the rest of the group for a moment while he cools down. "Okay. It looks like we're almost ready. Andy, would you get Ms. Avery for me?"

Strategies

Andy leaves the room while Mr. Sayre begins the math activity. He ignores Liz, who continues to sulk with her book. When Andy returns a minute later, followed by Ms. Avery, Mr. Sayre turns to her and says, "Liz needs to take a break in your room."

"Sure," Ms. Avery smiles. "Come on, Liz. We're going to my room for a bit."

Liz glares at Mr. Sayre and reluctantly follows Ms. Avery out of the room.

Ms. Avery and Mr. Sayre have agreed in advance to provide back-up to each other when a child needs to be removed from the classroom. Ms. Avery has a full-time assistant to help with a child in her room this year, and it is likely that she can come quickly while still leaving her own room in safe adult hands for a few minutes. In many schools, where single-adult classrooms are the norm, specialists or the librarian serve as buddies or the teacher calls the office for assistance.

Once the situation has escalated to this degree of conflict, the teacher does not engage with Liz further, nor does he leave the class to get help. Andy can get the help, while the teacher continues to teach the class. All the students get the message that the rules remain in place and their teacher will remain in charge.

Meanwhile, as Ms. Avery walks Liz to her classroom, she maintains a calm, matter-of-fact demeanor, not engaging Liz in conversation of any sort beyond telling her where to sit. Once Liz is settled, Ms. Avery returns to her regular teaching responsibilities. Later, when Mr. Sayre is free, he will come and bring Liz back to her own class to join the ongoing activity, letting her know that he and she will talk further later.

Strategy: Establishing Criteria and Self-rating

This strategy asks students to develop criteria for improving a troublesome situation, and then provides a very quick, efficient way for them to rate themselves based on the criteria they have developed. In the early weeks, we conduct frequent informal check-ins with students, requiring them to reflect and evaluate. This strategy builds upon, though does not replace, those informal check-ins. It is a useful way to concentrate upon a particular problem that affects the whole group.

After posting the agreed-upon criteria, the teacher conducts simple, predictable, and brief check-ins, with little or no discussion. For example, after lunch, a teacher might ask, "On our scale of 1 to 10, how do you rate Room 22's lunchtime today?" The teacher records the students' responses without comment.

Weeks Four to Six

The message to the children is that we trust them to take this quantitative feedback and apply it to the situation without a great deal of teacher intervention. The data is not the feedback of an authority figure, but reflects their own collective feedback. This strategy helps the process of self-regulation become tangible.

Strategy in Action

The fifth- and sixth-graders frequently return to the classroom from soccer time full of complaints. Some students "hog" the ball and never pass to the less-skilled players. Some yell angry put-downs at others when they make a mistake. Many argue with our volunteer coach, challenging his authority.

One day, after soccer time I hold a meeting. Rather than having the class air their complaints yet again, I ask, "If you are having a really fun soccer time, what is happening?"

We simplify the many responses into four statements describing a fun soccer time:

1. *The ball is passed to each player several times a game.*
2. *Players make encouraging comments to each other rather than put-downs.*
3. *Players do what the coach asks them to do.*
4. *Players accept the referee's calls without arguing or complaining.*

I post these criteria next to a large sheet of graph paper with numbers from 1 to 10 on one axis and the days of the week on the other. Each day after soccer, we go around the room with each student giving the class a rating for that day. I list the number as each child reports, then together we find the average number, and a child marks it on our wall graph.

Though this usually happens without discussion and is simply a time for feedback, the class begins spontaneously to set goals to achieve a certain number as they prepare to go to soccer. Though soccer time does not become perfect, it improves substantially, and the graph posts visible evidence.

Note that the teacher asked students to define behaviors that did make soccer work, rather than focusing on what wasn't working. There is a time for airing of complaints, and, in fact, it was the students' complaints which alerted the teacher to this problem. But too much time spent describing a problem or looking for its sources can lead to more resistance or disengagement on the part of those perceived as the offenders. Instead, the teacher assumed that the source of the problem was ignorance, insecurity, or bad habits, not purposeful ill will, and the group concentrated on visualizing and naming the behaviors of a great soccer game.

Strategies

Also, the soccer players themselves decided specifically what behavior they wanted to achieve and to what extent they had achieved it. Since the teacher did not even see the soccer games, the group knew that encouraging and evaluating their success was truly up to them.

Even when a teacher doubts the validity of a rating, he/she simply records it. For example, in the scenario above, one of the chief "ball-hoggers" once chose 9 while many classmates chose 4 and 5. The teacher did not need to question the boy's score. The average score spoke, and the message came from data, not from the teacher. It did not even come directly from individual classmates, and because the data spoke without judgment, the student was able to invest energy in self-correction rather than defensiveness.

Strategy: Apology of Action

The apology of action strategy requires a child who has hurt another child to think of an action that will help the hurt child feel better. Then, after the hurt party has agreed to the plan, the child carries it out. For example, a child who has made a hurtful comment might make a card listing nice things about the hurt child. Because the hurt child often asks for the apology of action, it provides a way to help students learn to stand up for themselves, as well as enabling more active reparation than a verbal apology.

This highly structured procedure encourages children to be respectfully assertive in the face of mistreatment, while it provides models for admitting and repairing mistakes with greater independence. Students initiate the action, come up with the plan, and complete it. This strategy involves students in the creation and application of logical consequences in the spirit of "you break it—you fix it," within the safety of the teacher's oversight and support.

For a thorough description of how a fourth-grade teacher introduces this strategy and teaches children how to use it respectfully, see the article in Appendix G titled, "Apology of Action: Teaching Children to Make Amends."

Strategy: Class Meeting

Class Meetings are whole-group meetings held for the purpose of problem-solving, or perhaps for planning a project or event which involves the entire class. They are held at regular intervals, often once a week, and have a particular format.

The highly structured and ritualized format of Class Meeting gives students regular opportunities to check in, plan events together, and problem-solve about classroom issues. It is best introduced after Morning Meetings are well under way, because the skills required for productive Class Meetings build upon the familiarity, trust, and communication skills established by Morning Meetings. While Class Meetings involve students in group problem-solving, the teacher's leadership role in preparing for and managing the meetings is key.

Weeks Four to Six

We recommend that Class Meetings include the following steps (Charney 1991, 80–85):

1. Introduce the problem or topic and review Class Meeting protocols. Use good listening, no "put-downs," etc.
2. Gather information. Go around the circle, eliciting short responses to carefully framed questions about the topic of discussion.
3. Begin discussion. Ask students what they think they might need in order to work on the problem or event/project.
4. Students brainstorm possible solutions and/or action plans.
5. Choose a solution and/or action plan. Evaluate each for workability and accordance with school rules.
6. When considering problems, choose a consequence. Name what will happen if the agreed-upon solution does not work, or if people do not keep to the agreement.
7. Close the meeting. Sum up the meeting, complimenting the positive efforts you have seen.

Items appropriate for Class Meetings should concern all or most of the class. At the outset, we select problems (though the problems may be suggested by students) that seem quite solvable or projects that are quite doable. We have facilitated Class Meetings with such topics as the following:

- There are never enough pencils in the pencil can, no matter how many we put out.
- Can we have an overnight field trip?
- Lots of kids have been arguing over games lately.

Through problem-solving Class Meetings, students participate in honest, nonjudgmental discussion leading to increased awareness, understanding, and empathy for their own behavior and that of others. They share ideas about what they need in order to change their behavior, then propose solutions and agree on one to try. In some cases, students propose and agree upon the logical consequence(s) for failure to follow the proposed solution.

Strategies

The following books are excellent resources on using Class Meetings:

- Charney, Ruth S. *Teaching Children to Care: Classroom Management for Ethical and Academic Growth, K–8,* rev. ed. Turners Falls, Mass.: Northeast Foundation for Children, 2002.
- Developmental Studies Center. *Ways We Want Our Class To Be: Class Meetings that Build Commitment to Kindness and Learning.* Oakland, Calif.: Developmental Studies Center, 1996.

Strategy: Conflict Resolution

Ritualized procedures for conflict resolution can help children resolve conflict peacefully and with a minimum of adult intervention. The communication skills developed in this process empower students to assert their feelings and experiences while maintaining respect for the feelings and experiences of others. Many good conflict resolution procedures have been developed and articulated in recent years. Most involve teaching children the following steps in some form:

1. Calming down (walk away, count to ten, etc.)
2. Explanation of the upset
3. Discussion and resolution
4. Some kind of acknowledgment (handshake, for example)

In our own classrooms, if a child wants to meet with a classmate for conflict resolution, we require that she/he must first compose an I-statement; then we arrange a time and place. Before teaching the steps of conflict resolution, we teach students to deliver emotion-laden information as I-statements, using the formula "When you _________, I feel __________, because ________, so what I would like is ____________________." We display this formula and practice, first, with positive, fun statements, such as "When you giggle, I feel happy, because it makes me giggle too, so what I would like is for you to keep on giggling." Next, we practice with statements containing more difficult emotions, working with examples removed from direct personal experience: "In *Charlotte's Web,* when Wilbur heard he would get eaten, he felt scared, because he didn't want to die, so what he would like is to be allowed to keep living."

Weeks Four to Six

We also generate a list of words, from literature as well as from our own experience, to expand our vocabulary for describing feelings—words such as scared, sorry, sad, angry, frustrated, nervous, irritated. Children glance at the list often when composing I-statements.

In a conflict resolution meeting, the first child makes an I-statement, and the second child listens, then repeats back his/her understanding of what was said. Once the first child agrees that the second has heard correctly, the second child may make an I-statement. The routine continues in which one child makes an I-statement, then the other repeats back what she/he heard (a simple form of active listening), until both (or all) parties feel satisfied that peace has been made.

In the early weeks, a teacher always attends conflict resolution meetings as a "fair witness" to ensure safety and protocol, but speaks as little as possible. As children become more adept, the teacher asks if either one would like a teacher's presence. If not, we leave them alone. We know that this approach to conflict resolution has become a part of our classroom culture when a student comes to a teacher and says, "Can we meet? I have an I-statement for you."

Strategy in Action

A solemn-looking Pearl approaches her fourth-grade teacher. "I have an I-statement for Robby," she says.

"Okay. Let's hear it," responds her teacher.

Pearl takes a deep breath. "Robby, when you said, 'Pearly, Pearly, silly girly,' I felt mad, because you were making fun of me, so what I would like is...so what I would like is..." There is a pause while she looks up at the poster with our I-statement formula while she searches to define what she would like. "I would like for you to call me 'Pearl,' not 'Pearly, silly girly.'"

"Sounds good," says her teacher. "I will meet with you both after lunch."

After lunch:

"Robby, Pearl has asked to meet with you," his teacher informs him matter-of-factly. "Let's go to the problem-solving table." Robby looks apprehensive and grins sheepishly at his buddy Mike as he accompanies his teacher to the table where Pearl is already seated.

Robby takes a seat, shifting nervously and looking sideways at Pearl as he chews a fingernail. Pearl sits up straight, glances at the wall chart, and clears her throat. Even with rehearsal, to speak directly of upset is no easy feat. Out comes her I-statement, exactly as she had practiced. As soon as she finishes speaking, Robby's words start to tumble out. "Well, she was..."

Strategies

His teacher interrupts. "Robby, you will have a chance for your own I-statement. Right now, it's time to tell Pearl what you heard her say."

"You don't want me to say 'Pearly, silly girly.'"

"Pearl, is that right?" asks their teacher.

"Yes."

"OK, Robby. Would you like to make an I-statement or end with a handshake?" His choices are clear and defined.

"I want to make an I-statement," asserts Robby. "Umm..." He glances at the chart for a cue. "When you said my new backpack was ugly...I felt...annoyed because...I like my backpack, so I would like...for you not to say it's ugly."

Pearl needs no cue. "You don't want me to say it's ugly?"

"Yeah!" comes Robby's emphatic response.

"Okay. I'm sorry." There is silence while Robby digests this apology. (While often a child will apologize spontaneously during a conflict resolution meeting, we never require apologies as part of this process.)

"Robby," asks his teacher quietly, "are you ready to shake hands or do you have another I-statement?"

The session closes with Robby and Pearl shaking hands. The handshake brings closure to the meeting, symbolizing that both parties have been heard and a mutual understanding has been reached.

Notice that Pearl's teacher listens to Pearl's I-statement before setting up the meeting. It is important for the teacher to have a preview of the issue and to make sure that the student has a legitimate I-statement. It is also important for the student to have practice saying it aloud. Though it may seem a simple and formulaic process, it takes great courage for students to initiate it and carry it through, and, in the meeting itself, it helps to have the starting words ready.

Notice, too, how many times Pearl and Robby both look to the chart for prompts. This happens not just in the beginning of the year but all year long. It's important to keep the chart clearly visible from the problem-solving spot.

Strategies for Academics

Curricula vary so widely from teacher to teacher and school to school that the following are intended as broad statements and strategies (with specific examples presented to illustrate the ideas) not as specific suggestions. The strategies should be translated and applied to the needs of individual classrooms. They can work with many different curricular approaches.

The content of the academic curriculum in the first three weeks has drawn largely upon the knowledge and skills students brought with them. Now we can work on new content and skills, while still allowing plenty of time for reflection on group process and behavior, role-plays, and practice.

If we have not done so already, we must assess skill levels in language arts and math, so that we can address the range of abilities more specifically and purposefully. The curriculum in reading, writing, and math moves from the open-ended guided discoveries and subsequent practice and elaboration to whatever curricula we will use for the year. By Week Six, we can usually expect to be able to focus our attention on an individual or a small group to teach new skills and content while the rest of the class functions responsibly with a reasonable amount of oversight.

We add to the basic knowledge we acquired in the first weeks through reading, field work, and other sources. We use topics we are studying to help us build a strong sense of classroom identity. A class might think of itself as the cricket experts, or the local historians, for example.

We look for opportunities to integrate our studies. A class studying beavers might do a Morning Meeting activity which uses creative movement to simulate beavers' swimming or building behaviors. While studying spiders, we read *Charlotte's Web* during read-aloud time, or teach the "Spider Web" greeting in Morning Meeting. A study of ratio and proportion in math can piggyback on a mapping unit in geography, culminating in student-created scale maps of our classroom or school yard. As we learn conflict resolution techniques, we might simulate a conflict resolution session between Native Americans and European explorers.

As we conclude topics or units of study in different curricular areas, we design culminating activities that often require collaboration. All class members might contribute to a "big book" on frogs, for example. Or small groups studying different regions of our country might work cooperatively to create murals representing their knowledge, with each member contributing an important element: people, animals, geographical features.

As children become increasingly familiar with expectations for behavior within the classroom, we can take advantage of opportunities for learning beyond the classroom walls. We may walk to a nearby library to see a local history exhibit, or go to the small patch of woods behind the school to collect leaves. We often give assignments that require students to use resources within our school building, asking questions of other teachers and school staff members, or polling other classes to gather data, for example.

Strategies

In these weeks, as students become familiar with more materials and techniques, inquire more deeply into content areas, and venture further afield, they continue to develop their identity—both individual and collective—as strong learners.

Show Shelf

Conclusion

"ORDINARY" MOMENTS

Children and teachers alike begin the school year with great anticipation—a late-summer mixture of excitement, anxiety, eagerness, trepidation, and hope. While the proportions vary from individual to individual, and even from year to year, depending upon many factors, it is a constant that the early weeks of each year offer particular opportunities and challenges. Fulfilling those opportunities and meeting those challenges require energy, creativity, deliberation, and careful planning.

In closing, we offer two glimpses into midautumn school life. We peek into small, ordinary moments that reveal children governing their own behavior in ways that make their groups function well as learning communities. These moments are "ordinary" because of all the hard, intense work done during the first weeks of school by both the teachers and the children of these classrooms.

Glimpse #1: A fresh morning message awaits the third grade as they enter their classroom. "Good Morning, Readers!" it says. "Today we will learn a new math game. We will also share something interesting about the books we are reading for homework. Below, write a word or draw a picture that tells something interesting about your book."

Brenda pauses at the door to say good-bye to her older brother, who walks with her to school every day, before he continues on down the hall to the fifth grade. She falls immediately into what is now a familiar routine. After hanging her jacket on her coat hook and depositing homework in its basket by the chart, she stands directly in front of the chart to read the morning message. Brenda, a bright, friendly, and often impulsive girl, struggles to read at a first-grade level. She gazes at the chart, making little sense of it. First her eyes, then her feet, wander. She notices that the teacher is busy talking to Fernando about a math paper. She scans the room and spots Amy choosing a math game from the shelf to play while she waits for Morning Meeting.

Many factors war within Brenda as she hesitates midway between the morning chart and Amy at the game shelf. She knows she is "supposed" to read the morning message first. She knows she needs help to do so, and that the teacher doesn't like to be interrupted when she's with a student unless it's urgent. Brenda would also like to be friends with Amy and sees an opportunity to spend time with her. Brenda also truly wants to learn to read better.

Brenda glances back at the chart. Justin, who Brenda knows is a very good reader, now stands reading it. With a last quick look in Amy's direction, Brenda retraces her steps to the chart and asks, "Justin, can you help me read this?"

"Ordinary" Moments

"Yeah, sure," replies Justin. "Just show me the words you don't know."

Glimpse #2: The kickball field rings with shouting, active fifth-grade boys and girls. Maria, who always describes herself as clumsy, has mustered her courage and decided to try kickball for the first time. She walks to the plate and swipes the ball with her foot when the pitcher rolls it to her. It rolls into foul territory.

"Good try, Maria! Just keep trying. You're gonna get it soon," Isaac, a star athlete, calls to his novice teammate. This supportive comment is very different from one that the highly skilled Isaac offered three weeks ago in a similar situation.

Maria kicks again, and this time the ball rolls right between the pitcher and third plate. Maria is so overcome with surprise that she stands frozen at home plate. She has been focusing so intently upon the connection between foot and ball that she hasn't really thought about the next step! "Run now, Maria, run!" yells Isaac, and both teams cheer as Maria makes it to first base, grinning with pride—and amazement!

Evan, a fierce competitor, comes to the plate next and kicks a hard pop-up ball right into the arms of the second baseman.

"Oh, that's the third out! Our team is up. Whose turn to kick first?" shouts the pitcher, as the teams run to switch sides and take up their positions without argument.

In addition to basic familiarity with the routines, what knowledge informed these moments in which the support of their community enabled children to take risks that would help them learn? In both scenarios, the children know quite a bit about each other. Brenda knows that Justin is a good reader. Justin knows that Brenda struggles with reading. Both know that it is OK, even encouraged, to ask for help and to give it. It is not "cheating."

The children also know the expectations for how they will treat one another. Isaac, along with his peers, knows that the definition of being a "good sport" in class play times differs from the competitive leagues he plays in on weekends. Maria understands that it is a goal for everyone to try unfamiliar activities, and that her efforts will not be ridiculed, even if her beginning attempts are awkward. Without this knowledge, these moments would very likely have gone in many different and less positive directions.

Conclusion

The way these students conduct themselves shows that the goals of the first six weeks are well met. These children know the routines of their day and the expectations for them, they know each other, and they use their knowledge to treat each other with helpfulness and respect. They do this when in the classroom, even though the teacher, while present, is not in immediate, direct supervision of the events described. They do this when they are on the playground under the supervision of a different adult. They have begun to internalize the expectations for the way they will help each other learn, and they are quite able to apply and translate the rules for community that they helped to frame.

Of course, even when the goals we outline for the first six weeks of school are accomplished, all does not proceed flawlessly from late October until June. The temptations to argue, to avoid difficult work, to let impatience and competitiveness lead to unkindness do not go away when the first six weeks of school end. However, most children, most of the time, can and will be resourceful, kind, and cooperative when led by adults who believe in their capacities and give them plenty of opportunities to learn and practice in the early weeks of the school year.

Appendix A

Samples of Morning Message Charts (K–6)

Key:

- Words that are in *italics* change each day.
- Underlined spaces (_ _) indicate letters or words that might be left blank for fill-in at Morning Meeting, either by the group or by an individual student.

Beginning of the Year

Kindergarten

Good Day!

Laura is first.
Raymond is the door holder.
Today is *Tuesday, September 12, 2000.*

We will fingerpaint.
What colors do you like?

First Grade

Dear Children,

Laura _ _ first.
Raymond _ _ the door holder.
Today _ _ _ _ _ _ _ _ _ _,
October _ _, _ _ _ _.

We will talk about our spider today.
Can you tell one thing you observed about our spider?

Luis' secret word is _ _ _ _ _ _

Samples of Morning Message Charts (K–6)

Middle of the Year

Kindergarten

Good Day, Children!

Thomas is _irst.
Maria is the _oor holder.
_oday is _ _ _ _ _ _ _ _ _,
February _ _, _ _ _ _.

We will write a story about our trip to the store.
Draw a food that you saw at the store.

Tameka's word is _ _ _ _ _ _ _ _ _

First Grade

Good Morning, *Mathematicians,*

Thomas is _ _ _ st.
Maria is the door hold_ _.
Today is *Th_ _sday,*
_ _ _ _ _ _ _ _ _ _ _, _ _ _ _.

Here is a math challenge for today:
4 + 4 + 2 + 2 =
Write your answer here ________

Tameka's secret message is _ _ _ _ _ _ _ _ _ _

Beginning of the Year

Second Grade

> Good Morning, Friendly Workers!
>
> Today is _ _ _ _ _ _ _ _,
>
> _ _ _ _ _ _ _ _, _ _ _ _.
>
> The shortcut way to write the date is _ _/_ _/_ _.
>
> *Laura* is first and *Raymond* is our greeting leader.
>
> *Yesterday we talked about how to invite someone to join in an activity with you today we will practice how to do this who remembers some friendly actions that you might use write your ideas here*
>
> *What's wrong with this message?*
>
> *Luis's* secret message says _ _ _ _ _ _ _ _
>
> _ _ _ _ _ _ _ _ _ _ _ _ _ _

Appendix A

Third–Sixth Grade

> Dear Friendly Workers,
>
> Today is *Monday, October 4, 2000.*
> *Thomas* and *Laura* will lead our greetings.
>
> *Our sharing this week is "Baby Memories."*
> *If you are signing up, remember to share a memory about you when you were a baby.*
>
> *Tomorrow we will start to do our "New Friend" interviews. Here are some ideas*
> *to think about:*
> *What is an interview?*
> *Why are we doing interviews?*
> *What might be a good interview question?*
>
> *Look at the underlined words. Be ready to tell how many syllables in each one.*

Middle of the Year

Samples of Morning Message Charts (K–6)

Second Grade

Good Morning, *Authors:*

Today is _____, 3/__/00.

Laura is first and *Raymond* is our greeting leader.

You and your partner will be given a special place to read. After you read, what are some questions you can ask your partner to help you talk about your story?

We will be reading our published books to the Kindergartners after lunch.

Third–Sixth Grade

Dear *Awesome Scholars,*

Today is *February 10, 2000* (_ _/ _ _/ _ _), and *Thomas* will lead our greetings.

The illustrations you did for our class read-aloud story are fantastic! The ideas they show are all so different. I want to display them all. Who would like to plan and arrange the display?

We are working on some math challenges today. Here's one sample for you to try:
2,435 – 1,569 = ________.
Be ready to tell what you did to solve it.

Syllable challenge: Choose a word for us to tell how many syllables it has.

Appendix B

Homework and the First Six Weeks of School

In the classrooms featured in this book, as in classrooms across the country, the amount and content of homework given varies a great deal, with much depending on the age of the students, the requirements of the school community, and individual teaching styles.

Whether students are expected to do homework every night from day one or are given periodic assignments throughout the year, there is much teachers can do during the first six weeks of school to greatly enhance the quality of the homework experience and ensure students' success. This is the time to "teach" homework, to introduce it slowly and carefully, to clearly establish expectations, and to take the time to practice the routine at school before children go home to do it independently.

In many schools, teachers devote time during these weeks to defining expectations for "good work" and teaching students how to do homework successfully. At the K.T. Murphy School in Stamford, Connecticut, for example, primary grade students complete all written homework in class for the first six weeks of school. Older students do so for the first two to four weeks. During this time, the students bring home their completed "homework" to share with parents, reinforcing the learning that occurred that day and connecting school lives with home lives.

The school-wide homework policy at K.T. Murphy is clearly communicated to parents along with expectations for quality work and suggestions for helping children meet these expectations. In the beginning of September, an information packet is sent to parents. The packet includes a letter explaining homework policy and procedures, a checklist of homework expectations, and helpful hints for setting up a work area and time for homework. A sample of this packet appears on the following pages *(reprinted with permission from K.T. Murphy Elementary School).*

Homework and the First Six Weeks of School

K.T. Murphy Elementary School

Lawrence Nichols, Principal
Marilyn Armengol, Assistant Principal

September 2, 1999

Dear Parents:

As we work to become more responsive to the needs of our students, we have developed a new K.T. Murphy Homework Policy. Time will be devoted each day to clearly define our expectations of "good work" and to teach our students how to do homework successfully. All written homework will be completed in class as follows:

- Grades K–2 for the first six weeks
- Grade 3 for the first four weeks
- Grades 4–5 for the first two weeks

During this time, your child's homework will be to bring home, share and explain these assignments to you. This will reinforce the learning that took place during the school day.

In addition, all K.T. Murphy students must read each night. Your child's teacher will send home specific details regarding at-home reading assignments. If at any time you are unclear about an assignment or have questions about your child's work, please contact the teacher. Don't wait until there is a crisis. Parents and teachers working together will insure that all K.T. Murphy students are successful learners!

As part of this new policy, we would like to encourage our students to choose a homework buddy, someone they can call if they have a question about an assignment, forget an assignment, or perhaps to quiz each other on spelling words. Please indicate below whether or not it is okay for your child to share his/her phone number with a classmate homework buddy.

Sincerely,

Lawrence T. Nichols
Principal

______ I understand the homework policy.

______ Yes, my child may share his/her phone number with a classmate homework buddy.

______ No, my child may not share his/her phone number with a classmate homework buddy.

____
Parent's signature

PLEASE CHECK OFF, SIGN AND RETURN!

SCHOOL
STAMFORD PUBLIC SCHOOL
K.T. MURPHY ELEMENTARY SCHOOL

A Stamford Public School in partnership with GE Capital Services

K.T. MURPHY'S

HANDY HOMEWORK HELPERS

HOMEWORK EXPECTATIONS

- ALL HOMEWORK SHOULD BE COMPLETED IN PENCIL.
- ALL WORK MUST BE LABELED WITH YOUR NAME AND THE DATE.
- YOUR WORK SHOULD BE NEATLY AND CAREFULLY WRITTEN SO THAT IT IS EASY TO READ.
- PAPER SHOULD NOT BE TORN FROM A SPIRAL NOTEBOOK AND SHOULD NOT HAVE JAGGED EDGES.
- KEEP YOUR HOMEWORK CLEAN AND UNWRINKLED.
- BE SURE TO CHECK OVER/EDIT YOUR WORK.
- WHEN WRITING, BE SURE TO USE YOUR OWN WORDS.
- REMEMBER TO ALWAYS DO YOUR BEST.

K.T. MURPHY'S

HANDY HOMEWORK HELPERS

HELPFUL HINTS

Homework and the First Six Weeks of School

WORK AREA

- Calm, clean work area
  ex: desk
  kitchen table
  bedroom
  livingroom (TV off)

- Bring homework supplies to work space

TIME

- Plan for: Homework time
  Break time
  Snack time

- Check homework folder daily

- Talk to your child about the homework

K.T. Murphy's

Handy Homework Helpers

Homework Supplies

- Pencils
- Crayons
- Scissors
- Glue
- Dictionary
- Erasers
- Paper

Please contact your child's teacher if you need help finding any of these homework supplies.

Suggestion for Keeping Supplies Handy

- Shoe Box
- Basket
- Baby Wipe Container
- Plastic Container

Appendix C

Games and Activities

Below are descriptions of the games and activities which are mentioned in the text. The games and activities are listed alphabetically. Each listing notes suggested grade level(s): primary (K–2); middle (3–4); upper (5–6).

See the Selected Bibliography for a list of our favorite games and activities books. These books describe many additional games, outdoor initiatives, and activities that are fun, that build community, and that foster active learning and participation.

A What? *(middle, upper)*

The children gather in a circle for this whimsical game. The first child hands a ball to the child on her left and says: "This is a dinosaur egg (or a grapefruit or a lollipop or whatever the child wishes to call it)."

"A what?" asks the second child.

"A dinosaur egg," says the first child.

"Oh, a dinosaur egg," says the second child, and he hands the ball to the third child. "This is a dinosaur egg."

"A what?" asks the third child.

"A what?" asks the second child.

"A dinosaur egg," says the first child to the second child.

"A dinosaur egg," says the second child to the third.

"Oh, a dinosaur egg," says the third child as she turns to hand the ball to the fourth child.

While the "dinosaur egg" goes around the circle clockwise, the other ball, perhaps a "golden ring," goes around the circle counterclockwise.

Blob Tag *(primary, middle)*

One person is chosen to be the tagger—the "blob." When someone is tagged, that person joins hands with the tagger and the blob grows. The blob grows bigger as more people are caught, and continues growing until everyone is one big blob. A variation is that the blob splits into two blobs once it becomes eight people long.

Bombardment *(middle, upper)*

You'll need two teams and a bounded playing field, which is divided in half by a rope, for this outdoor game. Three or more balls are placed on this rope. There is a back boundary marked at each end of the field.

At the start of the game, players run for the balls on the centerline and throw them, trying to hit opposing team members from the shoulders down. From the time the balls are in play, anyone may throw a ball if he/she can reach it from his/her half of the field. If a player is hit, she moves to the area behind the back boundary of the opposing team. If a player throws a ball that an opposing player catches in the air, then the player who threw the ball must count himself hit and move to the area behind the back boundary of the opposing team.

Any balls that can be reached from the back area may be thrown at the opposing team from the rear. The game ends when all the players of one team are behind the back boundary of the other team.

Captain's Coming *(primary, middle)*

"Captain's Coming" is played on a rectangular field, perhaps fifty feet long and thirty feet wide. The boundaries should be clearly stated, but they could be as rough as "in line with those trees over there."

This game has a number of commands called out at random by the "Captain," the teacher. There is a specific action applied to each command, and the last person or the last few people to perform the act are "out."

However, the trick for the Captain is to give some of the slower and younger children an advantage by calling out a series of commands before the person who is last is identified. For instance, the Captain might call "Land," requiring everyone to run toward the designated land on the far left of the field. Just before they reach the destination (with the older and faster children far in front), the Captain calls "Sea," and everyone must turn to run in the opposite direction toward the sea, which is on the far right side of the field. Now, the children who were slower to get to the land will have a head start on their trip to the sea.

Commands:
Land: Run to one end of the rectangle.
Sea: Run to the other end of the rectangle.
Port: Run to one side of the rectangle.
Starboard: Run to the other side of the rectangle.

Captain's Coming: Line up in the middle of the rectangle and face the Captain in a saluting position.
Man Overboard: Run to either side of the rectangle and look over the edge.
Abandon Ship: Piggyback with a partner.
Scrub the Decks: Pretend to be scrubbing the decks.
Climb the Rigging: Pretend to climb the rigging.

Capture the Flag *(middle, upper)*

"Capture the Flag" is a strategy game that can include many children. The play area is divided into two sections with lots of room for running. The children are split evenly into two teams, and each team is sent to one side of the play yard.

Each team has a flag (a handkerchief or piece of cloth) put in a designated spot and a jail that starts in a designated spot at the end of the play yard. Each team then chooses a guard to watch over its flag and over its jail (in very large games in a very large space, often there will be two guards—one for the jail and one for the flag).

Objective: To capture the other team's flag and bring it back without being tagged by the other team.

Capturing the flag: Children cross over the middle boundary line to try to grab the other team's flag. If the opposing team tags them, they have to join the jail line, which moves out from the jail point toward the middle boundary line. The children in the jail must hold hands, and each new jail member joins the line at the back. Children venture across the line often without getting the flag. If they are not tagged before they get back across the middle boundary line into their home territory, they are safe.

Points: When a team successfully captures the flag, that team receives a point; then both teams change sides and appoint new guards.

Guards: The guard is the only one who may stand back by the jail and flag. The guard must stand five giant steps away from both. Others may chase to the back line but may not stay there. It helps to change guards often and not wait for points to change.

Jail: A child can be rescued from jail by a member from her team who reaches the jail line and touches someone in it before being tagged by the opposing team. The rescuer takes the first person at the front of the line. They must walk hand-in-hand, and they are now safe to cross over the middle boundary line to their home territory. If the would-be rescuer gets tagged before reaching the jail line, then he must join the end of the line.

Category Snap *(middle, upper)*

The group sits in a circle in such a way that members can slap their own knees. A category, such as fruits, is chosen. The leader starts the rhythm which is some combination of a knee slap and hand clap that ends with a right-hand finger snap, and then a left-hand finger snap.

The leader begins by announcing the category on the right-hand finger snap (fruits) and naming one of the elements (bananas) with the left-hand finger snap. The next person in line is doing the rhythm with everybody else but must be ready to name the leader's fruit with the right-hand snap and then a new element in that same category with the left-hand snap. The play continues as so around the circle. Once an element has been named it cannot be used again. Try colors, states, basketball figures, singers, multiples of three, presidents, whatever.

Category Tag *(primary, middle)*

Taggers are all children who fit into a particular category. For example, the teacher announces a category such as "everyone with a hat on is it." Off go the "hats" chasing the "nonhats." If tagged, the nonhats must sit down to show they are caught. The game continues until all are caught. The game goes quicker and works better if there are clear boundaries.

The teacher then starts a new game with a new category, such as "everybody who is wearing jeans."

Chain Reaction *(primary, middle)*

This is a group discussion technique which ensures that every child speaks and that every child is heard. The children are gathered in a circle; the teacher asks a question or solicits a comment. Child one turns to child two and replies to the question. Child two turns to child three and replies to the question. This continues on and on, around the circle, until everyone has spoken and everyone is heard.

The Cold Wind Blows *(primary, middle, upper)*

This activity is a great way for children to learn about each other and to see what they have in common with classmates. Every person, except for one, needs to have a clearly marked spot in the circle (a chair, a book on the floor, etc.). One person starts in the middle and makes a statement such as "The cold wind blows for anyone who loves cats." Everyone who loves cats walks into the middle of the circle and then quickly finds a new spot in which to sit around the circle. There are two rules for finding a new spot: you can't go back to the same spot, and you can't go to the spot immediately to the left or right of your old spot. One person will end up without a spot and will stay in the middle to make the next statement: "The cold wind blows for anyone who plays the piano," or "likes to play soccer," or "has an older brother," etc.

It's important to stress that players name categories related to people's interests and backgrounds and not just to their clothing or appearance. It may be helpful, especially with younger children, to brainstorm a list of possible statements before the game begins.

Colored Dot Game *(middle, upper)*

"Colored Dot" is a good ice-breaking activity for the beginning of the school year. Children come into the room. The teacher places a colored dot (one of four to six possible colors) on each child's forehead. The child has not seen what color her dot is. Each child then has to find classmates with the same colored dot without speaking.

Continuous Kickball *(middle, upper)*

The field is set up like a regular kickball field but with only a home plate, a first base, and a pitcher's mound.

- An orange cone sits at home plate.
- A catcher stands behind the home plate.
- The remainder of the outfield is like a regular kickball outfield.

There are two teams. One team is lined up behind the home plate, and the other team has a player near first, a player as a catcher, and a player as a pitcher, while the rest of the players are out in the field. The pitcher's job is to try to roll the ball and hit the cone at home plate. The first player in line on the team that's up tries to kick the ball before it hits the cone at home plate.

If the kicker kicks the ball, she runs to first base, runs around it, and runs back to home plate. The object is to try to get back to home plate before the pitcher has another chance to roll the ball toward the cone and hit it.

- If the pitcher hits the cone, no matter when, the kicker is out.

- If the pitcher misses the cone when the kicker is running back to home plate, the kicker continues to run around home plate, out to first base, and then back, until the pitcher hits the cone. The catcher retrieves the ball when the pitcher misses the cone.
- If the kicker kicks a fly ball that is caught in the air, the kicker is out.
- When a team is up at "bat," the team gets three outs, and then the teams exchange roles on the field.
- Each inning a new student takes the pitcher's position.
- The ball always goes to the pitcher from the outfield. It is never thrown at the kicker or to the bases.

Games and Activities

Coseeki *(primary, middle, upper)*

"Coseeki" is a good game for developing observation skills. A child volunteers to be "it" and leaves the circle. While he is gone, a leader is chosen. This leader will lead the other children in a series of motions—a hand clap, a foot stamp, a head nod. The children sitting with the leader in the circle must watch the leader closely, out of the corners of their eyes, and repeat her motions.

The child who volunteered to go out of the room now stands in the middle of the circle and tries to guess who is leading the group.

Elbow Tag *(primary, middle, upper)*

In this tag game variation, after a child is tagged, he links an elbow with the tagger, and the two set off chasing together. When the next child is tagged, she too links an elbow, and the three of them set off on the chase. This continues until the last child is tagged. As always with a tag game, it is important to set the boundaries of the game before it begins. A variation is for the group to break into two tagging groups once it has become eight people long.

Electricity *(primary, middle, upper)*

"Electricity" is a nonverbal form of "Telephone." Children gather in a circle holding hands. One child sends a nonverbal "pulse" around the circle. This pulse passes from child to child until it returns to the first sender. *How long does it take? Can you beat your record? Can you beat the record from last year?*

The pulse can also be a nonverbal pattern: three little squeezes and a big one, or two big squeezes and one little one, or whatever. *Does the last child receive the pattern that the first child sent?*

Everybody Up *(middle, upper)*

Begin with two kids sitting on the ground, hands clasped, feet touching. Their job is to work together to raise themselves from sitting to standing. When two-somes succeed, students work in threesomes, foursomes, and occasionally even higher numbers.

Extended Name Tags *(middle, upper)*

Extended name tags are simply larger than usual name tags and include pieces of information about a person along with the person's name. Students are asked to draw a symbol or write a word representing something about themselves in each corner of the name tag. Here are some examples of topics for the corners:

- Your favorite place on earth
- Someone who taught you something
- A time you remember spending three great days in a row
- Something you love to do

Fish Gobbler *(primary)*

In this indoor or outdoor game, all you need is an area big enough for all the children to spread out with ample room to maneuver. When the caller (known as the fish gobbler) shouts "ship," all the children (the fish) run toward the wall (or marked boundary) to which he points. On the shout "shore," they quickly change directions and run toward the opposite wall (or marked boundary). On the signal "fish gobbler," the kids quickly drop to the floor on their stomachs and link arms, legs, or bodies together with one or more classmates. The fish gobbler moves around the room or playing field with arms outstretched swimming toward the other players but not touching any of them. The children are all "safe" as long as they are physically linked with someone else. Once the fish gobbler sees that everyone is linked to someone else, the signal "rescue" is called. At this moment, all the children jump to their feet, join hands, and yell "Yea!" raising their hands over their heads.

Various other calls could be added, such as "sardines" (everyone runs to a central point to make the tightest group possible by either lying on the floor or forming a massive standing hug); "fisherman all" (everyone sits on someone else's knee or knees); "crabs" (everyone backs up to a partner, bends over, and reaches under his own legs to hold hands); "fishnet" (let the kids use their imaginations and decide how to make one).

Follow the Leader ***(primary)***

The teacher, or a designated class "leader," performs a series of motions, goes on a walk to explore some area of the school (such as around the boundaries of the play yard or through the halls of the school), or simply makes different faces or hand motions. The children imitate and "follow" the leader.

Follow the Sound ***(primary, middle)***

Sounds are passed around the circle. Each child mimics the sound passed from the previous child, then creates a new sound to pass to the next child in the circle.

Four Corners ***(middle, upper)***

The group is divided into four teams. Each team retreats to its "corner" of a large square playing area. Each team is given colored flags (scraps of cloth) to tuck into their belts—no tying. Each team has a different color flag, and all members of a team have the same color flag.

At a signal, everybody heads for the diagonally opposite corner of the square. On the way there, anyone may grab anyone's flag. Once your flag is captured, your feet are frozen—you can't move. However, you are allowed to grab another's flag if she should venture too close. You are safe when you reach the diagonally opposite corner.

The game continues going from diagonal corner to diagonal corner on signal until the teacher decides it is time to stop. The team with the most members remaining at large (they still have their flags tucked in) is the winner.

Freeze Game ***(primary, middle, upper)***

Teachers use the "Freeze Game" to give children practice in freezing when a bell or other signal is sounded. The teacher invites the children to chat and move around the room. He then raises his hand, or rings a bell to signal that children should freeze. He counts to see how long it takes all the children to stop their bodies, look at him, and be quiet. The class is challenged to lower their time or perhaps to break a previous record.

Giants, Wizards, and Elves *(middle, upper)*

"Giants, Wizards, and Elves" is a variation on "Rock, Paper, Scissors" but is much more active. There are two teams and a playing field about forty feet long with a marked centerline. Each team agrees on a posture representing a giant, a wizard, and an elf and shows these postures to the other team. Each team huddles and decides which creature it will be. Teams come to the centerline and, at the count of three, assume the chosen posture and say the creature's name. Wizards fool giants; giants beat elves; elves trick wizards. Whoever loses has to run back to their safety, which is about twenty feet away from the centerline, before the other team catches them. Those caught become part of the other team.

Grandmother's Trunk *(middle, upper)*

The teacher begins by saying, "I am going on a trip, and I need to pack my grandmother's trunk." The first child then says what she will pack in the trunk. For example, "I am going on a trip, and I am taking my bike." Each child in the group then adds one item to the trunk, after repeating in order what is already packed in the trunk. "I am going on a trip, and I am taking my bike and my sneakers." The next child says, "I'm going on a trip, and I am taking my bike and my sneakers and my new Yankees hat." The next child says, "I am going on a trip, and I am taking my bike, my sneakers, my Yankees hat, and my toothbrush," and so on, until all the children have had a turn.

Group Juggling *(middle, upper)*

The children gather in a circle. One child holds a soft sponge ball or Hackey Sack®. He throws it to a second child, who throws it to a third. The ball is passed to each child in the group, until the last child throws it back to the first child. This child starts the "group juggle" all over again. After a few rounds, add another ball to the group and then a third. It can get quite challenging. Remember that each child always throws each and every ball to the same person she threw to in the first round.

Hospital Tag *(primary, middle)*

One or two people are "it," and another person is designated as the "doctor." When players are tagged by an "it," they continue to run around but must put their hand over the place where they were tagged (their wound). When someone has been tagged for the third time, he/she drops to the ground and calls "doctor, doctor." The doctor gently touches the person, which heals his/her wounds, allowing him/her to play again.

Hot and Cold *(primary)*

While a volunteer leaves sight of the group, another child chooses a place to hide an object. When the volunteer returns, she begins to search the room for the object while the class gives feedback. If the seeker is close to the object, they shout "hot!" and if far away, they shout "cold!" Gradations such as warm, lukewarm, and cool may be used as well. This continues until the seeker finds the object. It is good to have enough time for two or three seekers to find an object.

Games and Activities

Hot Potato *(primary, middle, upper)*

A hot potato (a ball, a Hackey Sack®) is passed quickly around the circle from one child to the next until a potato caller (who is outside the circle and facing the other way) calls out "Hot Potato!" The child with the potato in his hands at this time joins a separate "potato-callers" circle and chooses a number.

The potato is passed again while the potato-callers count softly to the chosen number. When the callers reach the number, they call out "Hot Potato!" in unison. The game continues in this manner until the last child has switched to the potato-callers circle, and all the other children have had a chance to select a "hot-potato" number.

Human Camera *(middle, upper)*

One partner is led blindfolded by the other to a spot. The leading partner focuses the blindfolded partner on a particular scene, such as a flower or landscape, and then *briefly* removes the blindfold so her partner can view the picture ("take the photo"). The blindfold is then replaced. Each partner may take several photos. At the end of each round, partners discuss the experience and share their impressions of the pictures taken.

Inchworm *(middle, upper)*

"Inchworm" is a close relative of "Everybody Up," described earlier. In this game, children are challenged to work with a partner to move across a given space while their feet and their hands are attached.

Jelly Roll *(upper)*

The object of "Jelly Roll" is to transport the entire group over an area covered with an imaginary poisonous jelly substance using only four large industrial paper tubes, which may touch the jelly, and a two-inch by ten-inch by twelve-foot board, which may not touch the jelly.

Solving this problem will require a high level of communication and cooperation—not to mention creativity! Make sure you step in to freeze the action and regroup the children if behavior and/or frustration levels appear counterproductive or harmful.

Kick and Catch *(middle, upper)*

"Kick and Catch" is a simple, fast game that kids love. You need a space divided in two, two teams, and a kickball. Team one kicks to team two. If team two catches the ball before it hits the ground, team two gets a point. Team two then kicks to team one; if team one catches, they get a point. Simple, fun, and quick. One important thing to pay attention to in this game is that the same children don't try to make every catch.

Kick the Can *(primary, middle)*

The person who is "it" stands by a tin can in the center of the playing area and counts to ten while everyone else scatters to find hiding places. The object is for someone to kick the can before being spotted by "it."

When the child who is "it" spots a player, she yells, "I see Jay behind the sandbox one, two, three." "It" must finish this whole sentence before the player gets to the can to kick it. If "it" finishes this call, the player goes to jail (a tree or a step works fine). If the player kicks the can, then that player becomes "it" next.

The following rules about jail are helpful: players need to be touching jail at all times or they can be accused of escaping; prisoners get five chances to escape for each game; when catching an escaping prisoner "it" only has to call, "I see you, Sam;" if a prisoner escapes successfully, he has to go to a new hiding place.

Knots *(middle, upper)*

Begin with a circle of eight to ten children who "knot themselves" by grasping right and left hands with random other hands in the circle. All hands must have another hand to hold. The children must then figure out how to unknot themselves without letting go of each other's hands.

Lean-To *(middle, upper)*

In this group challenge, everyone gathers in a circle and counts off by twos. The children hold hands in the circle and the "ones" slowly lean toward the center of the circle while the "twos" slowly lean back. Once this is accomplished, ask the "ones" to lean slowly back while the "twos" lean forward. It takes practice.

Line in a Snake *(primary)*

"Line in a Snake" is a fun way to travel through the school, go to the cafeteria, or explore the boundaries of the play yard. It is a traveling form of "Follow the Leader." The body of the snake always follows the head of the snake, wherever the snake goes. The children, with practice, learn to follow a designated leader. It is always best for the teacher to be at the end of the line so he has a clear view of what is happening.

Games and Activities

Memory Name Game *(middle, upper)*

The "Memory Name Game" is very similar to "Grandmother's Trunk" but is used to help children learn each other's names. The teacher asks a circle of children a simple question, such as "What is your favorite book?" or "What is your favorite food?" The children respond by stating their names and their favorite books or foods. For example, the first child might say, "My name is Jay and my favorite book is *The Table Where Rich People Sit.*" The second child would then say: "Jay's favorite book is *The Table Where Rich People Sit*. I'm Laurie and my favorite book is *The Little Prince*." On it goes around the circle, with children repeating everyone's name and everyone's book. If a child doesn't remember someone's name or favorite book or food, she simply asks that child to repeat it.

Mirror Image *(middle, upper)*

The teacher ask pairs of children to stand face-to-face. One child in each pair is the designated "mirror." This child observes his/her partner very closely and tries to imitate the partner's movements simultaneously, as though the partner were looking in a mirror.

Mother May I? *(primary)*

"Mother May I?" is a traditional game which most teachers will know from their own childhoods. One child or the teacher is the mother; all the other children line up facing the mother. There is a distance between the mother and the line of children. The point of the game is to be the first to tag the mother.

Children can move only when the mother tells them to, and even when she does tell them to move, they must respond with "Mother may I?" before taking the first step. For example, the mother might say, "You may all take two giant steps forward." The group would then call out, "Mother may I?" The mother responds, "Yes!" and the group takes two giant steps toward the mother. If any child forgets in her/his excitement to ask "Mother may I?" before taking the two steps, she/he must go back two giant steps.

Naming Challenge *(primary, middle, upper)*

The class is challenged to name everyone in the room, the unit, or even the whole school. This challenge may be issued to individual children or to groups of children who will act as a team. There must be times set aside to hear everyone's name and to practice attaching names to faces before the child or the team attempts to name everyone.

Nonverbal Birthday Lines *(middle, upper)*

This is a group challenge: *Can all the children in the room line up from youngest to oldest without speaking?* It definitely can be done, but it is not easy. The children could warm up for this challenge by first lining up by height or by first name in alphabetical order without speaking.

Octopus *(primary, middle)*

In this tag game, one child is the "octopus"—the octopus with long and dangerous arms. He is also the tagger. He attempts to tag another. When he does, that child is frozen, but she can wave her arms like the tentacles of an octopus, helping to tag others until all are octopuses. This game must be played with clear boundaries on all sides so that the untagged children are forced to move through the frozen octopuses.

Platform *(middle, upper)*

This is a group challenge in which the group attempts to get everyone in the class on a three-foot by three-foot platform or space. The effort is timed. If not done in twenty minutes, stop and debrief. Ask the children to talk about what is working and what isn't working. Then try it again on another day.

Popcorn Name Game *(primary, middle)*

The "Popcorn Name Game" is a circle activity to help children learn each other's names. Children go around the circle, popping up like popcorn, saying their name, "Hi! I'm Jeff," and sitting back down. Children should pop in order, and only one child pops at a time.

Red Light, Green Light *(primary)*

This is another old, traditional game. All children line up across the playground facing the "traffic light" (a teacher or a child chosen for this role). The point of the game is to be the first child to tag the "traffic light." The game begins when the traffic light yells "green light" and spins around so his back is to all the other children. The children run toward the traffic light. The traffic light then yells "red light" and spins around. Anyone whom the traffic light sees moving is caught and must return to the starting line. The game ends when someone tags the traffic light. The tagger then becomes the traffic light, and a new game begins.

Ra-di-o *(middle, upper)*

The class forms a circle, with room to form another circle on the outside as the game progresses. Each syllable of the word "Ra-di-o" has a specific arm and hand gesture that goes with it and that determines where the action will be sent next.

One person starts by saying "Ra" and puts either her left hand or her right hand above her head, pointing to the person on either the left or right side of her. That person says the next syllable, "di," and puts either his left or his right hand under his chin, pointing to the person on either his left or his right side. The next person says the last syllable, "o," and points to anyone in the circle, who then starts the action all over again by saying "Ra." The object of the game is to listen, be aware, and think about which action and syllable is needed, and not to make a mistake.

If a player does make a mistake, she goes out of the inner circle and begins to form the circle of "hecklers" who are on the outside of the circle. The hecklers have a very important job. They are to use words and sounds to try to distract the other players so that they cannot concentrate on the actions of the game. Hecklers may not stand in front of players or use their arms or hands to obstruct the players. Instead they may talk incessantly in a player's ear; they may sing at the top of their lungs; they may tell jokes or stories, etc. Pretty soon, most players are on the outside heckling, and there are very few on the inside trying to pass the action. The game can be ended before it gets down to the last player.

Safe Tagging *(primary, middle, upper)*

There are many terrific tag games. All of them, however, depend on the children's ability to be safe "taggers."

What does it mean to tag someone safely? Can you tackle someone? Can you dive at someone? These notions must be explored and defined with children before tag games are embarked upon. Discussions of what it means to tag safely should go along with the introduction of "tagger's choice."

"Tagger's choice" is a rule that simply states that if the tagger says you were tagged, then you were tagged. In tag games, arguments frequently flare up around whether or not a child was tagged. These conflicts can be held to a minimum if the tagger is always the one who "calls" the tag.

Scavenger Hunt *(primary, middle, upper)*

You can create a scavenger hunt almost anywhere. In a scavenger hunt, a series of clues are given to the children. The children are expected to "hunt" for the answers.

You start the hunt with a single clue. When you find the answer to that clue, you also find the next clue. Each answer leads you to the next clue until you have completed the hunt. The first individual or team that finds all the answers is the winner. Scavenger hunts can be used to explore the classroom, the school, or the playground.

Silly Soccer *(middle, upper)*

Soccer is a very simple and enjoyable sport for children. Almost every child loves to run and kick and try to score a goal. The trouble is that the faster and stronger children usually dominate. To solve this problem, try "Silly Soccer."

"Silly Soccer" uses the same basic idea of soccer in that competing teams attempt to score a goal by kicking a ball. However, in this version, there are three goals and no traditional soccer rules. The field is in the shape of a triangle, with a cone placed at each of the three points of the triangle. These cones serve as the goals as each team attempts to defend its own cone, without the use of an official goalie, while also trying to kick the ball so that it touches the other teams' cones. A team scores when a ball it kicked touches another team's cone.

With three teams and three goals, the game can get quite silly, and most players will quickly give up even trying to keep track of the score. A ball that is lopsided and rolls in unpredictable ways makes the game even more fun.

Games and Activities

Simon Says *(primary, middle)*

The teacher, or a designated class "leader," performs a series of motions, goes on a moon walk, or simply makes different faces. If the leader precedes his action by saying "Simon says," then the children are to copy the action. If the leader does not say "Simon says," the children are to remain still. If a child moves to copy an action that was not preceded by "Simon says," then, traditionally, the child sits down until a new game starts. If you do not wish to play a game where children are eliminated, simply start a second game and have children move between games. Instead of being eliminated, a child simply moves to the other game.

Smaug's Jewels *(middle, upper)*

One person is chosen as Smaug, a deadly dragon who stands guard over her jewels (a handkerchief or a piece of cloth). Everyone else forms a circle around Smaug and tries to steal the jewels without being tagged. Smaug can range as far from her jewels as she dares. If Smaug tags someone, that person is instantly frozen in place until the end of the game (games usually last about a minute).

Toilet Tag *(primary, middle)*

When a child is tagged in this game, he freezes in a squatting position, like the shape of a toilet, keeping one arm extended into the air until someone unfreezes him by gently pushing his arm down to "flush the toilet."

Zoom *(primary, middle)*

Children simply pass the word "zoom" around the circle one at a time. The child who begins it turns to her neighbor and says "zoom." Once the zoom is "received," the next person turns and passes it on. The first challenge is for everyone to pass the zoom flawlessly and smoothly around the circle. It might take a few tries! Once that is mastered, children enjoy timing themselves to see how quickly they can pass the zoom completely around once, then twice.

For more of a challenge, the word "eek" can be introduced to stop the "zoom" and reverse its direction. Whenever "eek" is said by the receiving child, "zoom" stops, reverses direction, and heads off the other way.

Appendix D

Greetings

The following greetings are either mentioned in the text or are particularly appropriate greetings for the beginning of the year. These greetings are easy to teach and to do, and many of them help children learn each other's names and interests. They are gathered from many classrooms and many teachers.

The Morning Meeting Book by Roxann Kriete has a number of these well-loved Morning Meeting greetings in Appendix D. *The Morning Meeting Book* is available through Northeast Foundation for Children.

A Simple Good Morning Greeting

A child turns to the child next to him/her in the circle, makes eye contact, and says, "Good Morning, ______________." The child greeted returns the greeting and then turns to greet the child on her/his other side.

Some variations:

- with a handshake
- with a "high five"
- with a pinky shake
- with a touch on the shoulder
- with a wave

Different Languages for "Good Morning"

Some options:

- Bonjour *(French)*
- Buon Giorno *(Italian)*
- Shalom *(Hebrew)*
- Buenos Días *(Spanish)*
- Ohieyo *(Japanese)*
- Guten Morgen *(German)*

- Jen Dobre *(Polish)*
- Jambo *(Swahili)*
- Kale Mera *(Greek)*
- Sign language

A Formal Greeting

Students greet other students using last names: "Good Morning, Ms. Cather," "Good Morning, Mr. Loman." Students sometimes find this fun because they feel a sense of importance being called by their last name.

Hello, Hello, Hello, and How Are You?

Greetings

This is a greeting used most often in the primary grades. It can be sung or chanted. The children form an inner circle and an outer circle at the meeting area. The inner circle stands still while the outer circle gradually moves around, so that each child in the outer circle eventually shakes hands with each child in the inner circle. As each pair shakes hands, they sing the following song:
Hello, hello, hello, and how are you?
I'm fine, I'm fine, and I hope that you are too.
Repeat as many times as you want or need to in order to have everyone shake hands.

Name Card Greeting

Place name cards in the center of the circle. A student chooses the top card from the pile and greets that person.

Introductions, Interests, and Favorites

Each child interviews a partner to prepare for this greeting.
"This is my friend _________, and his/her favorite activity to do is _________."
("and her favorite book is ___________.")
("and his favorite food is _____________.")
("and she/he is good at ______________.")

Pantomime Greeting

Each child pantomimes something about himself/herself (favorite activity, favorite food, favorite sport); others then greet the child and mimic the pantomime. The greetings are done by the whole class to each child.

Number Greeting

Place a slip of paper in a basket with a number on it for each person in the class. If there are twenty-four people in the class, put the numbers one through twelve in the basket, with each number appearing twice. The meeting leader walks around with the basket, and each person draws a number. The two people with number one come to the center of the circle to greet each other, and so on, until everyone has been greeted.

Skip Greeting

Each child skips a designated number of spaces and greets the person who sits that many spaces away from her/him. The child who greeted someone then sits in the place of the child who was greeted. The children greet and switch places until everyone has been greeted. Let the students figure out a good number of spaces to skip according to the number of students in the class that day.

Cross-Circle Greetings

Children greet someone sitting across the circle from them. There can be many variations on this, such as cross-circle boy/girl greeting, cross-circle someone-you-haven't-spoken-to-yet-this-morning greeting, etc.

Butterfly Greetings

There are two versions of this simple greeting:

- Sit-down butterfly: Two children sitting next to one another hook their thumbs together and wave their fingers in the sign language sign for butterfly while saying "Good Morning." This greeting then goes around the circle.
- Stand-up butterfly: This is the same basic greeting, except that students stand up and walk to greet someone across the circle.

Roll Call

"Roll Call" is a chant greeting used most often with older students (grades 5+).
Group: "Roll call, check the beat, check, check, check the beat. Roll call, check the beat, check, check, check a-begin."
Child says: "My name is ______________."
Group response: "Check!"

Child says: "They call me (nickname)."
Group response: "Check!"
Child says: "I'm a student. That's what I am." (Child chooses what to fill in here. Other examples might be "I'm a baseball player"; "I'm a poet"; "I'm a friend.")
Group response: "That's what (he/she) is."
And then the Roll Call begins again until each child has had a turn.

Greetings

Snap, Clap Greeting

A rhythm is established by the leader: clap, clap, finger snap (left hand), finger snap (right hand). Once the rhythm is going and all the children have it, the leader calls out her name on the left-hand snap and the next child's name on the right-hand snap. The next child calls his name on the left-hand snap and the next child's name on the right-hand snap. This continues around the circle until all the children have been named.

Spider Web Greeting

One child starts by holding a ball of yarn in one hand and one end of the yarn in the other. The child greets someone across the circle and gently rolls the ball of yarn across to that person while firmly holding on to the end of the string. The person who receives the ball of yarn holds a piece of the yarn down with one hand while greeting another child across the circle and rolling the ball of yarn to this child. This continues until everyone has been greeted, and the yarn has created a web across the meeting circle. To unravel the web, children greet each other in reverse order until the ball of yarn is wound up again.

Appendix E

Songs

Singing lightens our loads, singing cheers our day, and singing together makes us part of a community. Songs are an important part of many classrooms and an important component of the first six weeks of school. Below we list some of our favorite songbooks (with companion tapes or CDs) for classroom use:

- *I've Got A Song! A Collection of Songs for Youngsters.* Sandy and Caroline Paton. Sharon, Conn.: Folk-Legacy Records, Inc., 1975.
- *16 Songs Kids Love to Sing.* Collected by Northeast Foundation for Children. Turners Falls, Mass.: Northeast Foundation for Children, 1998.
- *Rise Up Singing: The Group Singing Songbook.* Edited by Peter Blood and Annie Patterson. Bethlehem, Penn.: Sing Out Corporation, 1992.
- *When the Spirit Says Sing.* Sandy and Caroline Paton. Sharon, Conn.: Folk-Legacy Records, Inc., 1989.

The following songs are mentioned in the text. Unless the song is traditional and in the public domain, it is referenced to one of the above resource books where you can find the words and music. All of these songbooks are available through Northeast Foundation for Children.

"Apples and Bananas," *When the Spirit Says Sing,* page 11.

"I'm a Little Piece of Tin," a traditional song. The words are:

> I'm a little piece of tin
> Nobody knows just where I've been.
> Got four wheels and a running board,
> Oh, I'm a Ford, Oh, I'm a Ford.
>
> Honk, honk, rattle, rattle, toot, toot, beep, beep
> Honk, honk, rattle, rattle, toot, toot, beep, beep.

"I'm Gonna Tell on You," *16 Songs Kids Love to Sing,* page 24.

"Peanut Butter, Grape Jelly," *16 Songs Kids Love to Sing,* page 16.

"Sandwiches," *16 Songs Kids Love to Sing,* page 14.

"This is a Song (Not Very Long)," *I've Got a Song!,* page 30.

"This Old Man," *Rise Up Singing,* page 178.

Appendix F

Read-alouds

Listed below are the read-aloud books that are mentioned in the text. We also list a few other powerful books to read aloud during the first weeks of school. Listings are alphabetical. Each listing notes suggested reading level: primary (K–2); middle (3–4); upper (5–6).

Some good resources for other books to read aloud include the following:

- Developmental Studies Center. *Reading, Thinking and Caring* (Gr. K–3) and *Reading for Real* (Gr. 4–8). Two excellent literature-based language arts programs. Oakland, Calif.: Developmental Studies Center.
- Hurst, Carol Otis and Rebecca Otis. *Friends and Relations: Using Literature with Social Themes, K–2*. Turners Falls, Mass.: Northeast Foundation for Children, 1999.
- Hurst, Carol Otis and Rebecca Otis. *Friends and Relations: Using Literature with Social Themes, 3–5*. Turners Falls, Mass.: Northeast Foundation for Children, 2000.
- Trelease, Jim. *The Read-Aloud Handbook*. 4th ed. Penguin USA, 1995.
- Wood, Chip. "Some Favorite Books for Different Ages." Appendix in *Yardsticks: Children in the Classroom Ages 4–14*. Expanded edition. Turners Falls, Mass.: Northeast Foundation for Children, 1998.

The Books

Primary

- Blood, Charles L. *The Goat in the Rug*. Aladdin Paperbacks, reprint edition, 1990.
- Dahl, Roald. *Fantastic Mr. Fox*. Puffin, 1998.
- Keats, Jack Ezra. *A Letter to Amy*. Puffin, reprint edition, 1998.
- Flournoy, Valerie. *The Patchwork Quilt*. E. P. Dutton, 1985.
- Havill, Juanita. *Jamaica's Find*. Houghton Mifflin Co., 1987.
- Peet, Bill. *Cyrus the Unsinkable Sea Serpent*. Houghton Mifflin Co., 1982.

- Seuss, Dr. *The Sneetches & Other Stories.* Random House, 1988.
- Viorst, Judith. *Alexander and the Terrible, Horrible, No Good, Very Bad Day.* Aladdin, reissue edition, 1987.
- White, E.B. *Charlotte's Web.* HarperCollins, 1952.

Middle

Read-alouds

- Cleary, Beverly. *The Mouse and the Motorcycle.* Avon, reissue edition, 1990.
- Binch, Caroline. *Gregory Cool.* Dial Books, 1994.
- Bruchac, Joseph. *The First Strawberries: A Cherokee Story.* Puffin, 1998.
- Bunting, Eve. *Going Home.* Harper Trophy, reprint edition, 1998.
- Dahl, Roald. *The Magic Finger.* Puffin, reprint edition, 1998.
- Jones, Terry. *Fairy Tales & Fantastic Stories.* Pavilion, 1999.
- Namioka, Lensey. *Yang the Youngest and His Terrible Ear.* Yearling Books, 1994.
- White, E. B. *Trumpet of the Swan.* Harper Trophy, 1973.

Upper

- Cooper, Susan. *The Dark Is Rising.* Aladdin, 1999.
- Curtis, Christopher Paul. *The Watsons Go to Birmingham–1963.* Bantam Books, reprint edition, 1997.
- Dahl, Roald. *Danny the Champion of the World.* Puffin, 1998.
- Fleischman, Sid. *By the Great Horn Spoon.* Little Brown & Co., reprint edition, 1988.
- Greenfield, Eloise. *Talk About a Family.* Harper Trophy, reprint edition, 1993.
- Lindgren, Astrid, and Alfred Lindgren. *Ronia the Robber's Daughter.* Viking Press, reissue edition, 1985.
- Lord, Bette Bao. *In the Year of the Boar & Jackie Robinson.* Harper Trophy, 1986.

Appendix G

Apology of Action: Teaching Children to Make Amends

By Mary Beth Forton

Reprinted from Responsive Classroom® *newsletter, Winter 1998, Teacher to Teacher article featuring fourth grade teacher Carol Davis*

It's mid-October in Carol Davis's fourth grade class and the children are drawing pictures of what they'll be for Halloween. Jonathan, Peter, and Lee, three friends, are working together at a table with a few others. Lee draws a beautiful picture of a pirate ship with seeming ease. Peter, sitting next to Lee, looks discouraged as he struggles to create something that resembles a vampire. After much erasing and sighing, Peter finally finishes and raises his picture triumphantly, "I did it!"

Lee takes a quick look and with a smile says, "Man that's ugly." Peter takes this as a compliment until Lee asks, "What is it?"

For a moment Peter seems confused as all eyes turn toward him. He looks across the table at his friend Jonathan who has just started wearing glasses. Peter lets out a quick, nervous laugh and announces, "It's Jonathan with his new glasses!"

Laughter erupts as Peter holds up the picture for everyone to see. Jonathan, tears welling up in his eyes, quickly stands up and walks away.

Scenes like this one in which children's feelings get hurt by their classmates are not uncommon in elementary school classrooms. While acknowledging that it's impossible to prevent every one of these incidents from occurring, fourth grade teacher Carol Davis has found a way to help students learn to stand up for themselves when their feelings have been hurt and to make amends when they have been the ones who have done the hurting.

Carol recalls a feeling she had several years ago which prompted her to try something new in her classroom. "I was tired of having kids leave school at the end of the day with hurt feelings and I was tired of feeling responsible for fixing these feelings when I wasn't even the one who caused them."

A Conversation

At this same time, while attending a *Responsive Classroom* workshop, she had a conversation with consulting teacher Chip Wood about Rules and Logical

Consequences. Chip mentioned that the rule, "you break it, you fix it," could be applied to hurt feelings as well as broken objects: when a child hurts someone's feelings, they do something to help fix these feelings. Carol was excited by this notion of an "apology of action" and immediately began planning a way to implement it with her fourth graders.

"The idea behind an apology of action made so much sense to me," Carol remembers. "I could recall so many incidents from my own life when I had done something that hurt someone's feelings and when saying 'I'm sorry' didn't seem like enough. Often I would do more. I'd write a note, I'd do a favor, I'd try to make amends."

Beyond "I'm Sorry"

Apology of Action

While Carol feels that saying "I'm sorry" is often appropriate and needed, she also feels that it's frequently inadequate. The process Carol uses for an apology of action not only gives the children who have done the hurting an opportunity to do something to make amends but it also gives the children who have been hurt the opportunity to stand up for themselves and assert their needs.

When introducing the idea to her students, Carol begins by telling them that we all make mistakes and hurt people's feelings, sometimes intentionally and sometimes without even knowing it. What's important, she emphasizes, is that we learn to pay attention to how our actions affect others and that we learn to take responsibility for these actions.

A Class Discussion

Carol starts with a class discussion in October. She asks her students, "How many of you have ever had your feelings hurt?" All hands go up. "What types of things have you done or seen others do that hurt people's feelings?" Eager to share examples, her class generates a long list:

- Laughing when someone makes a mistake
- Calling someone a name
- Ignoring someone during conversation in the lunchroom
- Telling someone they can't play at recess
- Making faces and rolling your eyes when someone is talking

Carol then asks her students to talk about how they feel when these things are done to them and whether an "I'm sorry" helps them to feel better. "Over and over, the children tell me that having those three words said to them doesn't do much to help them feel better." One child articulated it quite clearly when she said, "When someone says, 'I'm sorry', it doesn't take away the bad feeling inside."

"What would make you feel better when your feelings are hurt?" is the next question. "What if, for example, someone laughed when you made a mistake, what could that person then do to help you feel better?" She doesn't expect there to be any simple answers. Rather, what's important at this point is that the children begin to think about the question.

"You Break It, You Fix It"

Carol explains that in her classroom they'll be using the "you break it, you fix it" rule (which by now the children are very familiar with) when people's feelings get broken. "If you hurt someone's feelings, you'll have the chance to make it up to them by doing something for that person that helps to fix these feelings. We'll call this an apology of action."

In addition to learning to take responsibility for their actions, Carol wants her students to learn to stand up for themselves when they have been hurt. "Some children are afraid to speak up when someone does something that hurts them. This process encourages them to do so, which is especially important for the kids who are not as assertive," says Carol.

A Procedure

Here's how it works. In the above scenario, Jonathan's feelings were hurt by Peter. *After walking away from the table and taking some time to calm down, Jonathan approaches Peter and says, "You hurt my feelings when you said that about your picture looking like me with my new glasses." Peter apologizes and says he was only kidding. "I want an apology of action," says Jonathan.*

Sometimes children are able to ask for this on their own; at other times they need support from the teacher. Now, Peter has until the end of the day to decide upon an appropriate action.

Choosing an Appropriate Action

The most important guideline for choosing an apology of action is that it's related to the hurtful behavior. Take, for instance, the time when a child had been excluded from a game and the proposed apology of action was to draw the child a nice picture. Through a brief discussion with Carol, the child responsible was able to see that this action was not related to the hurtful behavior and instead decided to invite the classmate to play with her at recess on the following day.

In October, the class generates a list of possible actions which are left on the wall all year. Many of the students use this list as a starting point, something to refer to when they're having trouble coming up with an appropriate action.

Follow-Through

Apology of Action

In the beginning, Carol keeps track of the incidents so that she can make sure there is follow-through. "I jot down on post-it notes who owes whom what so that I can hold my students accountable. I want to send them a clear message that this is important and that I will expect them to follow through with it." As the year goes on, her students become more independent and

This chart and others like it are created by the children and left on display all year. Students use it as a springboard for ideas when trying to think of an appropriate apology of action.

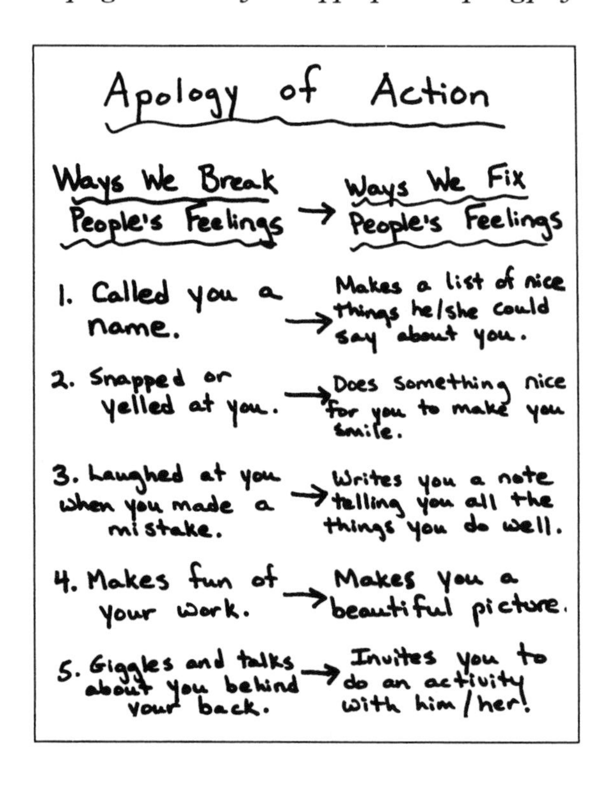

it becomes the responsibility of the child who has been hurt to make sure there is follow-through. Still, Carol remains watchful to make sure the process is being used well. Are the children being respectful and reasonable in their requests for an apology of action? Is the giving being done in a real and generous way?

Tagger's Choice

To prevent arguments about whether or not someone's feelings were hurt, Carol uses a rule from tag games called "Tagger's Choice." This rule states that if the tagger says you've been tagged, then you have. Similarly, if someone says that you've hurt their feelings, then you have. Carol explains to her students, "Lots of times we hurt other's feelings and we don't even know it. Whether we intend to be hurtful or not, we still need to take responsibility for how our actions affect others."

It's the end of the day and Peter stops Jonathan in the hallway to tell him that he has decided to draw a picture of him and write an apology on the back. He has already talked with Lee who has offered to help make the drawing look "really cool." Peter waits for Jonathan's response. According to class rules, the person who has been hurt needs to give their okay to the plan. Jonathan's thumbs up lets Peter know he likes the idea and the two walk together to their lockers to get ready to go home.

Selected Bibliography

The following are resources which we find particularly helpful for getting the school year off to a good start. We list resources for establishing a climate of trust and respect, for creating rules and routines, for building community, and for fostering active learning and participation. We also include our top ten games and activities books which we draw from frequently during these first six weeks and throughout the school year.

Selected Bibliography

Creating a Caring Community

- Establishing a climate of trust and respect
- Creating rules and routines
- Building community

Charney, Ruth Sidney. *Habits of Goodness: Case Studies in the Social Curriculum.* Turners Falls, Mass.: Northeast Foundation for Children, 1997.

Charney, Ruth Sidney. *Teaching Children to Care: Classroom Management for Ethnical and Academic Growth, K–8,* rev. ed. Turners Falls, Mass.: Northeast Foundation for Children, 2002.

Dalton, Joan and Marilyn Watson. *Among Friends: Classrooms Where Caring and Learning Prevail.* Oakland, Calif.: Developmental Studies Center, 1997.

Developmental Studies Center. *Blueprints for a Collaborative Classroom.* Oakland, Calif.: Developmental Studies Center, 1997.

Developmental Studies Center. *Ways We Want Our Class To Be.* Oakland, Calif.: Developmental Studies Center, 1996.

Gibbs, Jeanne. *Tribes: A New Way of Learning and Being Together.* Santa Rosa, Calif.: Center Source Publications, 1995.

Judson, Stephanie, Ed. *A Manual on Nonviolence and Children.* Philadelphia, Penn.: Nonviolence and Children Philadelphia Yearly Meeting, 1982.

Kriete, Roxann. *The Morning Meeting Book.* Turners Falls, Mass.: Northeast Foundation for Children, 1999.

Letts, Nancy. *Creating a Caring Classroom: Hundreds of Practical Ways to Make It Happen.* New York: Scholastic, 1997.

Porro, Barbara. *Talk It Out: Conflict Resolution in the Elementary Classroom.* Alexandria, Va.: Association for Supervision and Curriculum Development, 1996.

Prutzman, Priscilla, Lee Stern, M. Leonard Burger, and Gretchen Bodenhamer. *The Friendly Classroom for a Small Planet: Children's Creative Response to Conflict Program.* Philadelphia, Penn.: New Society Publishers, 1988.

Sapon-Shevin, Mara. *Because We Can Change the World: A Practical Guide to Building Cooperative, Inclusive Classroom Communities.* Boston, Mass.: Allyn and Bacon, 1999.

Selected Bibliography

Fostering Active Learning

Berger, Ron. *A Culture of Quality: A Reflection on Practice.* Providence, R.I.: Annenberg Institute for School Reform, Brown University, 1996.

Doris, Ellen. *Doing What Scientists Do: Children Learn to Investigate Their World.* Portsmouth, Mass.: Heinemann, 1991.

Fraser, Jane and Donna Skolnick. *On Their Way: Celebrating Second Graders as They Read and Write.* Portsmouth, N.H.: Heinemann, 1994.

Levy, Steven. *Starting From Scratch: One Classroom Builds Its Own Curriculum.* Portsmouth, N.H.: Heinemann, 1996.

Sobel, David. *Beyond Ecophobia: Reclaiming the Heart in Nature Education.* Great Barrington, Mass.: The Orion Society, 1996.

Sobel, David. *Mapmaking With Children: Sense of Place Education for the Elementary Years.* Portsmouth, N.H.: Heinemann, 1998.

Strachota, Bob. *On Their Side: Helping Children Take Charge of Their Learning.* Turners Falls, Mass.: Northeast Foundation for Children, 1996.

Walmsley, Sean A. *Children Exploring Their World: Theme Teaching in Elementary School.* Portsmouth, N.H.: Heinemann, 1994.

Wood, Chip. *Time to Teach, Time to Learn: Changing the Pace of School.* Turners Falls, Mass.: Northeast Foundation for Children, 1999.

Games and Activities

Fluegelman, Andrew, Ed. *The New Games Book.* Tiburon, Calif.: The Headlands Press, Inc., 1976.

Gregson, Bob. *The Outrageous Outdoor Games Book: 133 Group Projects, Games, and Activities.* Torrance, Calif.: Fearon Teacher Aids, 1984.

Luvmour, Sambhava and Josette. *Everyone Wins! Cooperative Games and Activities.* Philadelphia, Penn.: New Society Publishers, 1990.

Moore, Gwen Bailey and Todd Serby. *Becoming Whole Learning Through Games: Developing Your Child's Brain Power, Motivation & Self-Esteem.* Atlanta, Ga.: Tee Gee Publishing Company, 1988.

Orlick, Terry. *The Cooperative Sports & Games Book: Challenge Without Competition.* New York: Pantheon Books, 1978.

Rohnke, Karl. *Silver Bullets: A Guide to Initiative Problems, Adventure Games & Trust Activities.* Beverly, Mass.: Wilkescraft Creative Printing, 1986.

Rohnke, Karl. *Cowstails and Cobras II: A Guide to Games, Initiatives, Ropes Courses, & Adventure Curriculum.* Dubuque, Iowa: Kendall/Hunt Publishing Company, 1989.

Swartz, Larry. *Drama Themes.* Portsmouth, N.H.: Heinemann, 1995.

Vecchione, Glen. *The World's Best Street & Yard Games.* New York: Sterling Publishing, 1989.

Wiswell, Phil. *Kids' Games: Traditional Indoor and Outdoor Activities for Children of All Ages.* Garden City, N.Y.: Doubleday & Company, 1987.

REFERENCES

Charney, Ruth S. *Teaching Children to Care: Management in the Responsive Classroom*. Turners Falls, Mass.: Northeast Foundation for Children, 1991.

Charney, Ruth S. "Guided Discovery: Teaching the Freedom to Explore." In *Off to a Good Start: Launching the School Year,* 37-43. Turners Falls, Mass.: Northeast Foundation for Children, 1997.

Clayton, Marlynn K. and Chip Wood. "Rules Grow from Our Hopes and Dreams." In *Off to a Good Start: Launching the School Year,* 16-23. Turners Falls, Mass.: Northeast Foundation for Children, 1997.

Denton, Paula. "Choice in the Middle Grades: Keeping Play Alive." *Pathways*. Bethesda, MD: (May 1994): 8-12.

Developmental Studies Center. *Ways We Want Our Class To Be: Class Meetings that Build Commitment to Kindness and Learning*. Oakland, Calif.: Developmental Studies Center, 1996.

D'Nealian® Handwriting. Handwriting curriculum with series of grade-level practice and review workbooks. Glenview, Ill.: Scott Foresman–Addison Wesley, 1998.

Doris, Ellen. *Doing What Scientists Do: Children Learn to Investigate Their World*. Portsmouth, N.H.: Heinemann, 1991.

Fraser, Jane and Donna Skolnick. *On Their Way: Celebrating Second Graders as They Read and Write*. Portsmouth, N.H.: Heinemann, 1994.

Gibbons, Gail. *Caves and Caverns*. New York, San Diego, and London: Harcourt Brace and Company, 1993.

Gootman, Marilyn E. *The Caring Teacher's Guide to Discipline: Helping Young Students Learn Self-Control, Responsibility, and Respect*. Thousand Oaks, Calif.: Corwin Press, Inc., 1997.

Investigations in Number, Data and Space®. K–5 math curriculum developed at Technical Education Research Center (TERC), Cambridge, Mass., with the support of the National Science Foundation. Columbus, Ohio: Scott Foresman, 1998.

Kriete, Roxann. *The Morning Meeting Book.* Turners Falls, Mass.: Northeast Foundation for Children, 1999.

Levy, Steven. "To See the World in a Grain of Sand." *Educational Leadership* 57 (1999): 70–75.

Mackenzie, Robert J. *Setting Limits in the Classroom.* Rocklin, Calif.: Prima Publishing, 1996.

McCloskey, Robert. *Make Way for Ducklings.* New York: The Viking Press, 1941.

Nelsen, Jane. *Positive Discipline.* Revised Edition. New York: Ballantine Books, 1996.

Sitton, Rebecca. *Spelling Sourcebook Series.* Scottsdale, Ariz.: Egger Publishing, Inc., 1997 (There are several books in this series. Call 1-888-937-7355 for information).

Wood, Chip. *Time to Teach, Time to Learn: Changing the Pace of School.* Turners Falls, Mass.: Northeast Foundation for Children, 1999.

ABOUT THE AUTHORS

Paula Denton, author of *The Power of Our Words: Teacher Language That Helps Children Learn*, began teaching children in 1982. She began working as a *Responsive Classroom*® consulting teacher in 1990 and later managed program development at Northeast Foundation for Children. She has an MEd from Antioch New England Graduate School and an EdD degree from the University of Massachusetts.

Roxann Kriete is the author of *The Morning Meeting Book*. She taught in classrooms from grades five through high school before directing the publishing efforts of Northeast Foundation for Children and later serving as that organization's executive director.

ABOUT THE *RESPONSIVE CLASSROOM*® APPROACH

This book grew out of the work of Northeast Foundation for Children, Inc. (NEFC) and an approach to teaching known as the *Responsive Classroom* approach. Developed by classroom teachers, this approach consists of highly practical strategies for integrating social and academic learning throughout the school day.

Seven beliefs underlie this approach:

1. The social curriculum is as important as the academic curriculum.
2. How children learn is as important as what they learn: Process and content go hand in hand.
3. The greatest cognitive growth occurs through social interaction.
4. To be successful academically and socially, children need to learn and practice cooperation, assertion, responsibility, empathy, and self-control.
5. Knowing the children we teach—individually, culturally, and developmentally—is as important as knowing the content we teach.
6. Knowing the families of the children we teach and encouraging their participation is as important as knowing the children we teach.
7. How we, the adults at school, work together to accomplish our shared mission is as important as our individual competence: Lasting change begins with the adult community.

More information and guidance on the *Responsive Classroom* approach are available through:

Publications and Resources

- Books, CDs, and DVDs for teachers and school leaders
- Professional development kits for school-based study
- Website with extensive library of free articles: www.responsiveclassroom.org
- Free quarterly newsletter for elementary educators
- The *Responsive*™ blog, with news, ideas, and advice from and for elementary educators

Professional Development Services

- Introductory one-day workshops for teachers and administrators
- Week-long institutes offered nationwide each summer and on-site at schools
- Follow-up workshops and on-site consulting services to support implementation
- Development of teacher leaders to support schoolwide implementation
- Resources for site-based study
- National conference for administrators and teacher leaders

For details, contact:

Responsive Classroom®

Northeast Foundation for Children, Inc.
85 Avenue A, Suite 204 P.O. Box 718
Turners Falls, MA 01376-0718
Phone 800-360-6332 or 413-863-8288
Fax 877-206-3952
www.responsiveclassroom.org

LEARN MORE ABOUT RESPONSIVE CLASSROOM® PRACTICES

The Morning Meeting Book

By Roxann Kriete
with contributions by Lynn Bechtel

For K–8 teachers (2002) 228 pages ISBN 978-1-892989-09-3

Use Morning Meeting in your classroom to build community, increase students' investment in learning, and improve academic and social skills. This book features:

■ *Step-by-step guidelines for holding Morning Meeting* ■ *A chapter on Morning Meeting in middle schools* ■ *45 greetings and 66 group activities* ■ *Frequently asked questions and answers*

The Power of Our Words:
Teacher Language That Helps Children Learn

By Paula Denton, EdD

(2007) 180 pages ISBN 978-1-892989-18-5

Use your words, tone, and speaking pace with intention to help students develop self-control, a sense of belonging, and academic skills.

■ *The three Rs of teacher language: reinforcing, reminding, redirecting* ■ *Open-ended questions that stretch children's thinking* ■ *Listening and using silence skillfully*

Energizers!
88 Quick Movement Activities That Refresh and Refocus, K–6

By Susan Lattanzi Roser

For K–6 teachers (2009) 160 pages ISBN 978-1-892989-33-8

Give children two- to three-minute movement breaks throughout the day so they'll learn well.

■ *Chants, playful movements, short games, songs* ■ *Old favorites with new twists and original creations by the author* ■ *Can be used any time of the day, inside or outside* ■ *All energizers labeled by grade level and type*

Rules in School:

Teaching Discipline in the *Responsive Classroom*®
2nd edition

By Kathryn Brady, Mary Beth Forton, and Deborah Porter

For K–8 teachers (2011) 256 pages ISBN 978-1-892989-10-9

Establish a calm, safe learning environment and teach children self-discipline with this approach to classroom rules.

- *Guidelines for creating rules with students based on their hopes and dreams for school*
- *Steps in modeling and role-playing the rules* ■ *How to reinforce the rules through language*
- *Using logical consequences when needed*

Learning Through Academic Choice

By Paula Denton, EdD

For K–6 teachers (2005) 224 pages ISBN 978-1-892989-14-7

Enhance students' learning with this powerful tool for structuring lessons and activities.

■ *Information on building a strong foundation for Academic Choice* ■ *Step-by-step look at Academic Choice in action* ■ *Practical advice for creating an Academic Choice lesson plan*
■ *Many ideas for Academic Choice activities*

Parents and Teachers Working Together

By Carol Davis and Alice Yang

For K–6 teachers (2005) 232 pages ISBN 978-1-892989-15-4

Build school-home cooperation and involve parents in ways that support their children's learning.

■ *Working with diverse family cultures* ■ *Building positive relationships in the early weeks of school* ■ *Keeping in touch all year long* ■ *Involving parents in classroom life, including parents who can't physically come to school* ■ *Problem-solving with parents*